VISION QUEST

Native American Magical Healing

WOLF MOONDANCE

Illustrated by

THOM SEVALRUD

Sterling Publishing Co., Inc.
New York

To a dear loved one, Debbie White Eagle

Edited by Nancy E. Sherman

Library of Congress Cataloging-in-Publication Data available

10 9 8 7 6 5 4 3 2 1

Published by Sterling Publishing Co., Inc.
387 Park Avenue South, New York, NY 10016
© 2004 by Wolf Moondance
Distributed in Canada by Sterling Publishing
C/o Canadian Manda Group, 165 Dufferin Street
Toronto, Ontario, Canada M6K 3H6
Distributed in Great Britain by Chrysalis Books Group PLC
The Chrysalis Building, Bramley Road, London W10 6SP, England
Distributed in Australia by Capricorn Link (Australia) Pty. Ltd.
P.O. Box 704, Windsor, NSW 2756, Australia

Manufactured in the United States of America
All rights reserved

Sterling ISBN 0-8069-7207-6

Acknowledgments

My heartfelt thanks go to my mother, Marie Screaming Eagle (November 5, 1919–October 15, 1994), for her belief and dedication to her vision. To the staff at Seven StarLodge, www.wolfmoondance.com, for their hard work and belief in Rainbow Medicine. To the students and staff who walk to the medicine to find their inner spirit.

Each one of you over the last 30 years has been a true pleasure and joy to work with. For the ones who have opened doors so that I could walk in the vision world, I give thanks: to Running Water; to the man who fishes; to the stick being; to Lightning Raven; to Little Red Wolf; to Fading Deer; to Dancing Spirit; and Grandfather Bear Heart; to the one with blue eyes. I thank you for being a part of Vision Quest. I thank you for your admiration and commitment.

To Grandmother/Grandfather Spirit, thank you for giving us a mind that can see in the Spirit World. Love to my half-side Raven, for flying out in front and watching over, for holding onto everything in a good way. Thank you for showing me the morning skies.

To Sheila Anne Barry, my editor, for help in editing and guidance; you open doors for me to want to write so I have to live...thank you.

Thank you to my loving nephew Tyler for your hard work on this book, your quick eye and magic fingers. XO...

Contents

Preface

Are we alone, blinded, living in an existence that is kept from us, hidden in the secrets of our thoughts? Are we to live as physical beings and never really know what that means? Do we wander around from one religion to another, seeking the advice of this teacher and that minister and this preacher and that priest, and this rabbi and that shaman? Are we on this earth simply to grow up, marry, have children, grow old, and die? Or is life an adventure? Do we have a choice?

Are we scared that we don't know what our choices are and where they came from? Are we reaching out for answers, turning to our computers, our textbooks, our philosophies, our professors? And are we still lost?

Maybe we are motivated only through sugar use, drugs, and alcohol. Maybe we don't have anything to hang onto in our lives except for the things someone has given us, saying they were family jewels or traditions. Why do we have names that were passed on to us when we don't even know the people who gave them to us? What is it about our lives that we want to live in the first place?

The answers to those questions and many more are in *Vision Quest*. I will take you to a place where you will come to understand your vision. Vision questing is very, very old, and more than just one race of people have used it.

When you go on a vision quest, you are seeking to understand something that is simple, like a cloud. When you hear a sound in the darkness, you will know it's a voice guiding you. Vision questing comes to me as a Native American because of my mother, Marie Screaming Eagle, who was an Indian—as Native Americans are called in America. She was a holy person in my eyes, and in our community's eyes, for she knew the answers to the questions I've just asked you.

The biggest questions people ask are "Who am I?" "Why was I created as a human being?" "What is my purpose on Earth?" Many people come together in wisdom and knowledge of their clan, nation, or tribe, seeking to answer these questions. Some of us are alone. Some of us have been abandoned, left to be adopted by anyone who might care. Some of us are wounded. Some of us have healed ourselves magically.

What's a magical healing? Why is a vision quest a magical healing? I learned from the teachings of my mother that in all Native American tribes, we look beyond the physical world. We look to the spiritual world for guidance. We walk with the knowledge of teachers from the Spirit World. We live with spirit guides, with the knowledge of our animal totems, with the teachings of the animal clan, the animal spirit guides that direct us in life, as well as the spirits themselves. They bring magical healing to our existence.

I am going to tell you about four of my students who walked with me in the time of Vision Quest. You will see the doors of the Spirit World open to these students. We will walk within a time in this book where you can begin to create your own vision quest. There are several different vision quests a person can take, among them, solo vision quest, the woman's vision quest, healing vision, and youth vision quest.

It is important to understand that the magical healing of a vision quest is a personal thing. It is a personal pathway, your vision quest, which opens the door to your spiritual and physical wholeness.

You need to journal the vision and either seek help in learning from it, or sit and take the vision apart to bring its meaning to your life. I hope that this book will offer you ways to understand your vision. We as humankind have a hard time with visioning, because we think we are just having a dream. But the vision is a path that will help guide you to the life you want.

SOLO VISION QUEST

In the solo vision quest you make your own rules about what you want to quest for and where you wish to do it. No one sets any conditions or guides you but your inner spirit and your spirit guides, if you are in touch with them, along with Great Spirit/Creator/God.

When you take a solo vision quest, you go on your own. You set the place and the time. You can quest in your home but you must have no one in the house at the time—no pets or family members. There are four important questions to ask yourself when doing a solo vision quest.

1. What knowledge of vision questing do you have? Have a clear understanding of what you are looking for.
2. What will the vision quest do for your daily life? How will you apply the vision to your personal life on a daily basis?
3. After you have a vision, what do you do? Work with the vision and make an outline so that you can follow the vision and understand your spiritual path.
4. What will you do to take your self to a higher level of understanding of your vision and the path you will follow because of the voice of the vision?

Getting a teacher of vision quest and learning a lot more about your vision is the right direction to take.

THE WOMAN'S VISION QUEST

The woman's vision quest is done when the woman is getting ready to ask for her mate. She goes to an elder woman who knows the way of this quest and they set out to vision her mate. This quest is also done when it is time to have a child. There are four important questions to be answered before this quest is undertaken.

1. Is the woman ready to call forth the spirit of her mate?
2. Does the woman have permission from her elder or parent or teacher to walk as a woman of age, of knowing, and of wisdom?
3. Does the woman know how to pray to see the answers in the Spirit World—pray open and clear—and say that she has made a mistake and that that is okay?
4. Is the woman ready to call the soul of her child to flesh and see the child grow to be all that it can be in this life and live the lesson Creator gives the child?

HEALING VISION

The healing vision is done at home in a spot that feels safe and warm. You do this to see the sickness you are dealing with.

Sit and listen, and in your mind you will see, hear, or feel the sickness. As you do, coat the sickness with a silver color; so it looks like glitter. Take four deep breaths and let the sickness be released. Pray for your knowing that you are safe and strong. Pray for a change of the ways you have that might be making you sick. Hear the ways that are making you sick and list them and how you are going to live in a new way. Visualize yourself making changes in what you do that makes you sick. As you close the vision of healing, see yourself well.

YOUTH VISION QUEST

There is a traditional way the Native Americans take their young on a vision quest and that is personal to each family. I teach a youth quest in four parts.

1. Age 7.

The children are to sit with their parents and talk of the spirits and Great Spirit. They are to be given a clear understanding of the family's knowledge and belief in Great Spirit/Creator/God, including the needs and wants of the family. Teach the children to see a dream and a vision as a picture in a book. Teach them to see clearly—to have the picture clearly in their minds. Then, with a special blanket—the child's medicine blanket—have them sit and think. Have them listen to the parent pray for their vision to be shown to them. Let them sit until they see a vision in a clear picture. It will come soon. Ask as the children sit, "Do you see your vision?" Children will tell what they see. Record what they see in the children's vision journal and have them draw the picture they see in their minds. It's okay for the picture to be very primitive.

After the vision, praise the children and tell them they have their spirit vision and they will remember the vision. Then start to work with the vision by getting them to talk about what they saw. Study the parts of the vision from the picture they have drawn, and bring it to life as a part of their life. Let them have objects such as rings, necklaces, and drawings, fetishes that represent parts of their vision.

2. Rites of passage, age 13.

The family gathers together to work with the second phase of the youth vision. The children bring the picture of the vision and their vision journal. It is very important that the children have written down everything they have experienced in their vision from age 7 until they turn 13. Allow the children to express their feelings about their vision. Then take them to a quiet place—preferably outdoors at dawn, where they will not be disturbed—and leave them with their medicine blanket. Instruct them to pray and to look for their vision. The vision will be very clear to them. Tell them they are to listen and think about the vision guiding their life until they are 21. The picture of the vision they have had stays the same, but they will see and hear things they need to add to their vision journal. If they experience new guardian animals or totems, it is to be understood that they are new spirit guides for the second part of their vision.

3. The youth's connection to his or her vision at age 21.

This is a time where the young person is instructed to take a 24-hour solo vision quest. The youth takes his or her vision journal and the picture of the vision and goes to a quiet place outdoors, preferably in the wilderness. This may also be done in the quiet of the home, but there can be no people, phones, or pets for the 24-hour period of visioning. The youth sits with his or her vision and answers the following questions in the vision journal.

a. Does the vision show me who I am to marry or what kind of family to have?
b. Does the vision show me the type of vocation I am to follow?
c. Does the vision show me the location I am to live in? (Clues may come from the animals and where they live, the surrounding area in the vision—ocean, mountains, desert, etc.)
d. As I reflect on my vision, what stands out the most?

Whatever stands out is telling me the direction of my life path and can answer any question I ask.

4. The youth vision moves on into maturity.

If you have started your children with a youth vision, when they are between 21 and 24 years of age, they go out on a four-day vision quest to sit with their vision (the picture they have had over the years) and ask the Great Spirit to open their minds to communication with their vision. During this time, they write in their vision journal anything new about the picture or the spirit guides or animal totems they have. It is now time to follow it as an adult vision and apply the teachings of any typical vision quest.

Encourage them to experience the feelings that go along with questing.

LEADING A VISION QUEST

There are many different ways for vision teachers to lead a vision quest. I want to share with you things and ways that I believe are important:

1. Vision quest teachers should have their personal vision, and should have had it at least five years earlier. A leader needs to have had his or her own teacher of vision questing, someone who has worked with the facts of their vision and has taught the meaning of the vision.
2. At the very least, the leader must be a person of high moral quality. He or she must have a clean police record, with no illegal drug use or alcohol abuse, no sexual exploitation of a student or other sexual problems, no problems with anger, and no control issues.
3. Leaders need a staff to help with teaching, and the qualifications in rule two above apply to these assistants as well. They too must have personal visions and apply them to their daily lives. The staff is there to help with ceremony and supplies, and to make the students comfortable and safe.
4. Leaders need to provide a safe, quiet, private place for a vision quest.
5. Teachers need a recognized ability to interpret symbols, animals, plants, herbs, and stones, along with a strong under-

standing of the Spirit World and spirit guides. They need knowledge and experience with different vision quests, from many races and beliefs.

6. Leaders need the knowledge to be a name-giver, and to have studied the different ways of archiving tribal names and the gifting of a spirit name.

7. There is a strong need for knowledge of human development, psychology, and psychiatry, as well as spiritual beliefs. It is very important for leaders to see themselves as teachers of vision and not changers of the students' personal ways.

8. Leaders need to believe the vision quest is a pan-cultural experience, recognizing the human need to integrate deeply the internal change necessary in times of transition. Within sacred time and space, they help the student focus on letting go of the past, connecting to nature, and entering the Spirit World to seek clarity and vision. This is a time for acknowledging our unique contributions to life, to validate who we are, and to confirm our place in the community.

When you find your vision, it will be one of power and beauty. It will give you the feeling of Great Spirit and of hope and guidance.

From the vision, a magical healing will take place. When you follow your vision as I teach it, you will encounter new opportunities and experiences that bring forth your intensity, your impeccability, your intention, and the realization of the meaning of your existence.

I feel it is very important that you understand why you want to vision quest. What is it you wish to discover? Are you looking for your purpose in life?

One of my favorite medicine words in the vision quest is "mystery." Could it be that you are looking for the mystery of your wholeness? What if you are suffering from religious persecution, or self-abuse, or family abuse? Your vision will enable you to open the door to your total self, not what someone else wants you to be, but who you know you are.

When you experience a vision quest, you are confronting the power of the sacred circle. You are freeing yourself from your fears and coming into your total power to understand the spiral of life.

We all have emotions. When we embark on a vision quest, we encounter our seven primary emotions: acceptance, disgust, happiness, sadness, anger, fear, and joy. A human is made of emotions acting out in a physical form. When you go to get a vision, you face your emotions—which are your fears. As you find your vision, you begin to understand them. When you live with your vision, they become clear in your life. A vision quest brings you truth and balance and helps you to recognize your purpose.

You can miss your vision totally by being in the emotion of anger. It is very important to have clear vision and to understand the vision, you must understand your fears.

The vision is a way of life that will help you to reach your fullest potential of magical healing. First you see your life as it is, and then the vision opens you to symbols, colors, pictures, and guides from the Spirit World that may totally redirect the path you are on. You will be able to make changes that take you to the joy and acceptance you seek.

Vision Quest: Native American Magical Healing is a contemporary teaching. It is my vision—the one that I, Wolf Moondance, walk and teach at my lodge. But a vision is a personal thing and each of us needs to experience our own vision and the freedom it can bring. There are tribal ways to do visioning, but in the end it comes down to the individual to find his or her vision, live his own life, and follow the voice of Creator.

I have led vision quests for over 20 years, assisting students to walk the rainbow path and find their magical healing. Every individual has the right to quest for the inner self, to embark on the sacredness of his or her vision.

✳   ✳   ✳   ✳   ✳

I extend to you now the opportunity to set your intentions, find your path, confront your fears, and set yourself free. Follow the sky path to the stars and listen to their song. I like to think that as you reach for the stars, you will heal your scars, that magical healing will come from your personal vision quest.

If you are looking for your true self, only you have the answers. It is a rite of passage you are seeking. A vision quest will bring you to the path of spirit. This is the way to find and know your purpose and understand the choices you have in life.

The message of the vision will need to be interpreted. I have included here as many of the meanings of things as I can so you can find the truth of your vision. It might take many years to comprehend your personal vision completely, but you will have a strong guide to lead you. The journey to your vision will be a wonderful and magical trip.

Aho.

THE SACRED ACT OF SMUDGING

For as long as I can remember, I have heard of smudging with sacred herbs such as tobacco, sweetgrass, sage, and cedar. There are a lot of reasons why it is a good thing to smudge, either with one of the sacred herbs or all of them together.

In the first place, tobacco was a gift of the Four Spirits of the Four Directions. It was Great Spirit who gave us tobacco, a symbol of peace. Thereafter, the people smoked the Pipe of Peace before great councils, after war, and before other ceremonies. It is said that tobacco chases away feelings that are bad or negative and brings on good or positive thoughts.

In the second place, tobacco was in the nature of incense, sweet to the taste and fragrant to smell.

Cedar was offered to the fire to smudge the lodge and people. It is also used to waft the smoke about to ward away sickness.

We gain knowledge with our tobacco and we grow spiritually. Our hearts feel and our spiritual eyes see what our Creator wants us to learn. We feel the knowledge in our soul, and we know it comes from our Creator. When we pray, we get answers; we are nurtured and we grow spiritually.

Smudging with the four sacred herbs mentioned—tobacco, sweetgrass, sage, and cedar—helps us center ourselves. Burn clippings of the herb in a clay bowl or shell. If the herb is bundled in a "wand," light the end of the wand that isn't woody and use that. I like doing it this way. Direct the smoke with your hands or with a feather wand.

It is a good practice to smudge each person in a group, circle, ceremony, and lodge. Starting from the East and holding the lighted smudge pot, each person bathes him- or herself in the smoke. Many people smudge the heart area first, next the head, then the arms, and downward toward the legs. This isn't the only way you can smudge. Any way you choose to smudge is appropriate.

After smudging the individuals, smudge the room, slowly walking clockwise around its perimeter, fanning the smudge pot, keeping it lit, and wafting the smoke about.

Offer reverence to the four directions, moving the wand in a clockwise motion. While doing this, say:

To the East—Eagle, the spirit of all life.

To the South—Coyote, the child and youth in all.
To the West—Bear, the introspection within the self.
To the North—Wolf, the wisdom to guide and teach.
To Father Sun.
To Earth Mother.

Smudging should be done with care, with reverence, with an attitude of love. It shows respect and honor toward the plants that Creator has provided for healing; the plants will return the favor by keeping you well and free from disease and negative energy.

Feel free to purify and cleanse often, an especially good idea these days, when there is so much sickness and so many bad feelings around. It isn't ever wrong to smudge.

Smudging is done in the vision quest as each student goes off to vision and then again when they return to base camp. It is done with a prayer and a blessing.

SAGE

Sage is burned in smudging ceremonies to drive out evil spirits, negative thoughts and feelings, and to keep negative entities away from areas where ceremonials take place.

Sage has long been acknowledged as a healing herb, as is reflected in the fact that its genus name, Salvia, comes from the Latin root word salvare, which means "to heal" or "to save." Several varieties of each genus are used for smudging, such as S. apiana, commonly known as white sage, and Artemisia, known as sagebrush, which is more common in the wilds of California. There are many other varieties, and all are effective in smudging.

SWEETGRASS

Sweetgrass is burned after smudging with sage, to welcome in good influences after the bad have been driven out. Very important to the Sioux and Cherokee nations, its botanical name is Hierochloë odorata. In these tribes, the sweetgrass is braided and burned by lighting the end of it. Sweetgrass is very rare today, and traditional Plains people have been attempting to protect the last of it.

CEDAR

Many trees are special, but cedar may be the most special of all. When people were new and first learning their responsibilities and discovering things they ought not to know, cedar was used to bless the home and all who came in contact with it. Cedar works both as a purifier and as a way to attract good energy. It clears negative emotions and is great for healing.

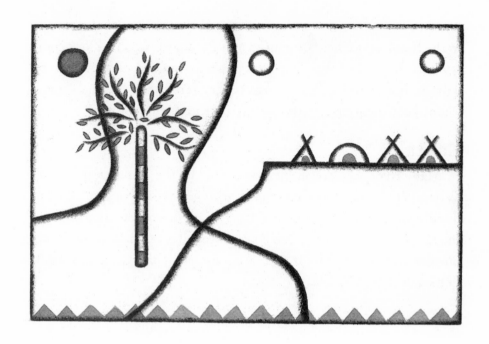

· 1 ·

Four Students Are Chosen for the Vision Quest

I want the wholeness I seek. I cry for the teachings of spirit. I seek the shaman to find the answers. Why was my childhood so hard? Why so much pain? Will those spirits answer me? I call to the Wolf to teach. I drift off in the night sky listening to the shimmering stars. The answers await me and I seek the morning. It is hard to wait. Where will I go from here? Is this where the answers wait?

—John

John is from Cleveland, Ohio. He is 29. He had a hard childhood.

His father was a child abuser and killed his brother when John was 12. His father went to prison, leaving John to be the head of the family. His mother's brother moved in and the home was one of crime and abuse. John saw lots of drinking and stealing by his uncle and mother as they tried to run the family. He had to work and bring home money. His love was basketball, but there was no time for it. There were no spiritual teachings in the home.

In our Lodge, the Seven Star Spiritual Lodge, I teach vision quest. There is a strong need to have a personal vision. I was given my vision when I was very young. My mother taught me to listen and live from the teachings of my vision.

As I grew, the voice of the vision led me to all the things I wanted in life. I learned to be in contact with wise ones and they taught me to know the ways of my vision. Each student who comes to his or her vision will open the door to answers and knowledge from the Spirit World. To each person comes to the lodge to vision quest, I teach the vision ceremony from the voice of my vision.

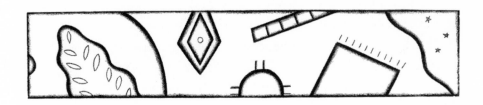

My assistant Pepper Dog appears with a stack of papers. "Wolf, these are from people who are ready to go for their vision quest. They all completed the studies you assigned them and there are four you should probably look at—John, Lee, Cathy, and Linda."

Pepper Dog hands the papers to me and I hold them, look at them. There are many, but I have room for only four on this trip.

"Why are you giving me so many?" I ask.

"There are several students who have worked very hard and they're ready to go. There are others who feel that they're ready. These are the ones that you can choose from."

Vision quest is a good experience. It is an endeavor in which people come together to complete one of the most important journeys of their lives and, as teachers and assistants, we have the satisfaction of guiding them. What are they questing for? They are seeking their whole selves through Native American magical healing. They are turning to alternative healing ways. Vision questing is not for everyone, for it is very deep spiritually and philosophically.

I look back at Pepper Dog. "Have we a support staff ready to go for this one?" I ask.

"We have people ready to go. Yes, Wolf, we can be ready at a moment's notice."

"All right."

I take the student applications and go to my prayer circle. I sit in my rocking chair while my prayer assistant Lightning Raven lights the candles. I watch the shimmering, golden light of the fire, hear the crackles and pops, and smell the pine and the hickory. The support staff, the ones with black hats, approach and sit.

"I have come to stand in confidence and support the work of those who need to seek." It is Jack Red Fox; he is wearing a red shirt. Jack is on the teaching council of Confidence. He is 31 and an ex-drinker. When his vision came to him, it changed his life. He has been with the lodge for 20 years, helping and working with the people and the vision fire. He is to assist with the meals and see that the water is brought to the students during vision time.

White Mouse came to the lodge for a vision when he was 18. He had lost his own family and become a son in ours. How time flies! He has been with us six years. His love and care for the people of the lodge is warm and strong, and we are very blessed to have him. He is the one in the orange shirt.

Butterfly Sky is a soft spirit I can call on to help and walk as staff any time. She was only 19 when she was called the first time, losing her sight in the physical world and full of fear. We worked together for five years; she worked with the healing vision and the doctors, and her physical sight started clearing up. She has opened her faith and now walks with clear sight.

"I have come to see that the prayer sticks are made, that the vision poles are proper, that the instructions of the vision are good. I have come to make sure that we have prayer ties and all the things it takes for the students do their vision pictures when they are finished." She speaks softly. She is wearing a yellow shirt.

Cat Eyes walks up. She is true green. I call her my real rebel; she fought and clawed for many years, trying to be in class and have a vision and yet hold onto the drink and drugs and sex. She called her actions her "wild side." She came to me when she was eleven years old. Boy, we had our work cut out! She tried five times to get a vision before she gave up the wild child and everything fell into place. She walks with the true beauty of a woman, and her green eyes perfectly reflect the vision with which she lives.

"I have come to watch over and stand by the road in prayer when they go forth from their vision quest, and I will be there to help them answer their questions about growth." She is wearing a green shirt.

I look up and see Making Words; he is the young one, only 18. A family who died left him to me in their will when he was one year old. He makes up words and we laugh and feel the power of joy in our hearts. I am "ole auntie" to him. I would be lost without his soft hands and sweet eyes. As he walks with the students, he has found the ways of truth to guide his life and open the path of spirit forever, he says.

"I have come to stand beside you, to hold the clipboards, to listen to your words, to hold your water bottle, to help you in any way I can, for you are the guide, and that is truth." He stands strong in a blue shirt.

The staff member in purple, Dancing Spirit, is the one with the question. She says if she has a question, I will always teach. Drinking, men, and drugs were her medicine for many years, but her vision of a dancing spirit set her free. She has been with us for 15 years and I have come to rely on her checking and typing and hard work. One of her spirit names is Coyote Face; it's good to have those who bring laughter. She takes the heavy edge off for the staff, who are under great strain, because we don't always know if the students will find their way.

"I have come to see that when we speak, they journal, and that what they see and hear is recorded in their spirit journals. I am here to help with wisdom."

✳   ✳   ✳   ✳   ✳

Pepper Dog nods and stands. She is wearing an impeccable shirt, one of burgundy. This is the highest color in the lodge. This color is earned with completion of all the studies of Rainbow Medicine and is given with my assent. This is when they are placed on my personal staff and work with the most intense ceremonies and healings that I offer as a teacher. Impeccable is one of the flawless nature teachings: there can be no mistakes, no anger, and no fear. It is perfect in itself and ideal in thought.

Pepper Dog hands me my own burgundy shirt with the word boss on it; the staff gave it to me as a joke. They said that it always takes someone to drive the mules, and that's the boss.

"We are a team," she smiles. "Once more, we're gathering a group and bringing them to sit in a vision square, where they can hear the impeccable truth of Grandmother/Grandfather/Great Spirit. I am here to see that they understand the process," she says.

The staff members are all sitting around the fire. Over their shoulders, I see walking toward us the four students who have come to seek their vision. They are hungry for knowledge. I watch them as they come closer. They are seeking their individuality, their intention, and they cry for inner strength and spirit wisdom. They long for their spirit names and the roads they need to travel to find the lives they so strongly seek.

I stand and say, "I can take only four, though there are many who have studied Rainbow Medicine and many other ways of the spirit."

I have a hard time when I get to this point—picking who will be the ones, but the Creator knows the ones who need. There are always more to go the next time, ones waiting to see their path.

"I wish we could take many, but this is the way—four."

I sit back down and hold their papers in my lap. Papers are earthly things that teach me, that show me their need. They speak of pain and lost ways. They tell me of actions that separate them from their spirit. Each student has kept a journal and answered questions I have given them so I will know how to aid in their vision and which spirits to call on to help.

I hold the papers in my hand and I pray.

"Grandmother, Grandfather, heya. Thank you for today. I pray for these four young ones who come to the wisdom, for it is so ancient. They are as small as dust, as you are as large as the sky. We come to feel the gentle kiss of the wind and the song of the stars, the guidance of the Earth, the visions of the fire. We know that as we turn loose everything in our past and open our hearts to wholeness, our total life lies ahead of us. We come for magical healing. We ask that you share with us in vision quest time the truth of our inner spirit. Thank you and bless our footsteps. Aho."

John, Cathy, Lee, and Linda. I look at the sheets in my lap. We will all be off on an adventure soon.

Pepper Dog says, "These four are a good choice."

"Yes, I'm ready to go to base camp," I say. "Are you ready for your experience?" I ask the students.

Each one answers yes.

"Are there any questions you would like to ask?" I say.

The words of John echo in my mind. "Why was my childhood so hard?"

It's interesting when people come and quest for their vision. They seek the answers to so many things. As I look into the morning sky and the sun kisses my cheek, I know Grandmother/Grandfather/Spirit will have the answer.

"John, the answer must be important to you and I know it will be answered by the spirit. Is this the reason you vision?"

"Yes, I must get past the pain and stop the self-abuse. Can the vision help with that?" he asks.

"Yes, if you balance your understanding with the realization that people hurt people because they have been hurt. It's up to you to stop the pain and self-hurt. The vision is a handle to hang onto and the key to setting your goals to walking a good life. Okay?" I ask.

He says, "Yes."

"Each of you is going on a vision quest. You will need to prepare your vision quest medicine bundle.

"This bundle is used to honor those from the Spirit World, as well as to bring honor to the Earth Mother and yourselves through learning respect for humankind.

"You will need tobacco. I recommend loose tobacco—the kind you roll cigarettes with. This is not for smoking or consuming; it is for gifting the Earth Mother. Tobacco is a sacred herb that enriches. You also need sage or cornmeal—it can be white cornmeal—to give to the Earth Mother for the spirits to consume, as well as the crawlies and others that walk the Earth Mother and want to eat."

VISION PRAYER STICK

"You need to make what we call a vision prayer stick, which provides a connection point between you and the Spirit World. It will help you focus and see (seeing is often knowing or having a feeling. Then the feeling becomes a want or a need) and hear in the Spirit World."

The stick is 2½ feet (75cm) long and about as big around as your thumb. You will need four pieces of cloth cut 1 inch (2.5cm) wide by 14 inches (35cm) long. The color of the first cloth is white. This will help you connect with the spirits of the Spirit World. The color of the second is blue to help you connect with the truth of your vision. The third cloth is purple, which helps you receive, interpret, and understand the knowledge of your vision. The fourth cloth is red, which helps you connect with the strength of your vision. You will need some string or sinew, to which you will tie your personal beads. You can use as many beads as you want, to show your connection to color and spirit.

Wrap your prayer stick in the four cloths. Also place a crystal on top of the stick—you can glue it on or just wrap it on the stick—to help dispatch your thoughts to Great Spirit.

Keep the stick wrapped in red cotton cloth when you are not using it. When you bring the stick out, smudge it. Then sit with the stick and pray about your vision and feel the power of the stick. In prayer, the stick will help you connect with spirits and the symbols of your vision. When you are done with the prayer stick, wrap it in the red cotton cloth and place it with your sacred tools on your altar. The stick will be helpful during your vision and at any time you wish to work with your vision.

"You will need fire to keep you warm," I tell the students, "and you will need a support group. The staff members are there to help you, watch over you, and keep you safe from wildlife, as well as passersby and others. You will need someone to cook food for you at the end of the vision quest. Each one of the staff—Pepper Dog, Cat Eyes, Making Words, Jack Red Fox, White Mouse, Butterfly Sky, and Dancing Spirit—will be there to help and give you the feeling of support.

"You will be going on a retreat vision quest; this is called 'out on the mountain.' The group will be at base camp, and then out in the wilderness for four days. Please speak to Pepper Dog to get a list of things that will be needed for the time you are out." I say.

"You need someone to drum, if you determine that you need drumming and can't do it yourself. You need someone to drive you to your vision quest, so that you can stay focused on your intentions and thoughts. You should also have someone to take care of you when you need water during your vision time and someone to help you return and re-enter your life when your vision quest is over.

"You need the prayer and the support of other people to make the vision quest a time of retreat in which you can seek out your higher self and understand the spirit part of you.

"It's good to have people with you whom you know well, who will take care of you and help to create a sacred setting. The way you set up camp is very important. It should be at least a mile away from where the vision quest will take place. The questing site itself is a quiet spiritual space that you will choose for yourself. The rest of your support group will stay back in the camp, set up with fire, food, water, drumming, and safety. The safety I speak of is respect. Vision questing is serious so there should be no noise, no joyful playing, and no interaction other than prayer and support for the vision quest."

THE HISTORY OF AND REASON FOR VISION QUESTS

Vision questing is a spiritual journey. You can undertake it in the wilderness, in the quiet of your home, or in a special place in a state park or by the ocean.

A lot of people think that vision questing is strictly Native American. It is a kind of retreat that has been common among our ancestors, our ancient spiritual traditions, and shamanism. But the vision quest is not only Native American; it is found in many, many ancient spiritual traditions. Any bloodline or tradition that claims to own vision questing—or says that it happens because of them— would have a hard time proving it. All peoples have their own form of taking sabbaticals and drawing within themselves. You find it in con-temporary shamanism, Earth medicine, Native American and Celtic traditions, and in studies of traditional—as well as contemporary—medicine wheels.

A vision quest is spoken of in the Bible when Jesus goes away for 40 days and, alone in the desert, studies himself. Vision quest is a time for you to look within and come to an understanding of your spirit self, and to fit that knowledge into your physical presence. It is a personal journey that you take to find your spiritual path and con-nect with yourself.

The ability to listen to your vision—the voice of your mind— is given to you by Grandmother/Grandfather/Great Spirit/ Creator/God.

I believe that vision quest is the seeking of knowledge that goes beyond our physical presence into a space we know as the Spirit World. We quest for spiritual knowledge just as we do for physical.

I believe in the spirit. Most Native Americans are taken on their first vision quest when they are children. My mother took me when I was five, and then we studied the vision for many years to help it become the map of my life. I set life goals from the map and I live them to this day.

What is the right time for you to go on a vision quest? The earlier in your life, the better. In any case, there comes a time, as you walk in your physical existence, when you must leave your friends, let your work go, and step away from physical callings. Then you walk within yourself to discover the changes within the sacred circle of life of which you are a part.

When you vision quest, you are taking a spiritual journey, a path that has been followed by human beings for eons. You hear a calling within yourself and you don't know what it comes from. You hear a pulsating question that pushes you to reach inside and explore the depths of yourself. Who am I? What am I doing with my existence? Why was I created? How can I heal my wounds and understand the purposes of anger and fear?

This call is from the star people, and they offer magical answers to awaken your life. Through your vision you are on a spiritual path of star knowledge, ancient knowledge that is available to all who answer the call.

Despite your fears, you have come to this place of sacred journey. My mother used to say that Native American vision questing takes you to a magical place where you open your mind to the spiritual. It is where you meet with others in the Spirit World. When you gain your vision, you will be on the path of spiritual healing.

In the healing, you let go of fear, and work on the spiritual aspects that make you human. It is no accident you are human. You will learn the terrain of the Earth Mother, whether you walk inside the wilderness, along the sea, or in the middle of a busy city. You will see—through your dedication, reverence, and respect—a physical center of safety, of survival, where your innermost secrets are revealed to you through ancient symbols, teachings, pictures, songs, and thought patterns.

When you take a group retreat, you will find that you become part of a small, strong community of people who offer support to each other. Group retreats are undertaken with a leader who is safe and available to support and comfort you. A good thing about the group retreat is the sharing that goes along with it. Your daily life, your home, friends, and work are left behind. You go to the Earth Mother and are with the spirits and the staff, your tools, and yourself.

Vision questing is a ceremonial rite of passage, and it doesn't matter from what bloodline or tradition you study it. What matters is to understand that a magical healing will take place once you open up to the new age and age-old ceremonial patterns that lie within your mind.

Vision quest is guided by the metaphysical concept of the medicine wheel. There are four quadrants: the spirit, the emotions, the physical, and the brain/mind. I like to see the vision quest as a telephone call from spirit, except we need no tangible, material phone.

When you go on your vision quest, you will have a close encounter with nature; you will become intricately interwoven within the spiritual knowledge and ancient wisdom of the winged ones, the crawlies, the swimmers, those that sing, the feathered ones, the standing peoples (the trees), and the grand masters—the mountains—along with the majestic beauty of the sun, moon, and stars.

We are all called at one time or another to ask the question why. We are all invited to understand the peace of mind we have been given from Grandmother/Grandfather/Great Spirit. It is important to put aside arguments, anger, lack of history, lack of comprehension, and understand that the vision quest will seek out every possibility that brings you closer to your inner questions and your inner knowledge. You go within the wilderness or sit in the quiet of a park or garden and let it mirror your soul.

Let it open you up to peace and expansion. The medicine wheel is a metaphor—a wheel with symbols and structures of teaching and human experience, and through intense understanding of it, the self unfolds. It shows us a deeper and more perfect, soul-directed way of life.

Through the vision quest, humankind has been guided by the stars and totems, which are the wilderness keepers, the crawlies, and the winged ones. If we listen, we can hear the voice of Grandmother/Grandfather Spirit whistling in the wind.

Aho.

SOLO VISION QUEST

Every vision is done solo, unless it is a guided vision, in which case it is a subject someone else wants you to see and feel. The solo vision quest I'm speaking of is done on your own with nothing but the following teachings, which are designed to help you set up your own vision at home or anywhere else you wish to go. It is important that you not be interrupted, that you set a period to be alone.

I know that often you hear that you must fast, must do the vision quest for a certain length of time, go to a certain place, or be under the supervision of a teacher. I feel all you need is to define the word "vision" and "quest" and go for it. I had a student say to me, "You mean you make it up? You just make your vision as you want it to be?"

Everything is made up. It is called creativity, thinking, thought, or idea. So don't put so much pressure on yourself. As you set out to find your vision, remember Creator and that spirits are real and want to teach and visit with you.

As you go on your vision, make sure you are comfortable, quiet, and undisturbed. A solo vision can happen fast, but I think it is best to set 24 hours apart from your daily world and go to a place where you are totally alone.

You may want to take a blanket to cover yourself and a hand drum to play to center yourself. A special spiritual rock or prayer cloth (this is a rock or cloth with a painted symbol on it, used during prayer) or any other sacred tool may go along to be used as you vision.

It would be good if, as night falls, you keep all lights off and use candles as you work. You need a journal and pen to keep notes of what you see and hear. You will need to sketch your vision when it comes—the simpler the drawing the better.

STEPS OF A SOLO VISION—MOONDANCE VERSION

1. Meet your inner spirit.
2. Feel spiritual energy.
3. Connect your spiritual life with your human life of now.
4. Meet your spirit guide.
5. See your vision.

1. Meet your inner spirit.

a. Sit with your eyes closed. Relax and see nothing but darkness.
b. Tell yourself you want to see your spirit.
c. Think of a place that is calm and pretty where you can sit down.
d. Watch and you will see someone or some being walking toward you.
e. Look at the being and remember what you see.
f. Open your eyes and journal what you saw. This being is your spirit self. After you write what you saw, you need to interpret the spirit self.

Example: You see colors, yellow and green floating. You might see a wolf with stars around it. (Any thing you see—animal or thought—is right.) Whatever you see, you need to interpret. You also need to identify the smells and sounds you experience.

This is how you get to know your spirit.

2. Feel spiritual energy.

a. Sit and breathe and relax.
b. Close your eyes and stay relaxed. Feel nothing. With eyes closed, rub your hands together real fast. You will feel your energy rising, and the heat climbing.
c. Before you, with eyes closed, you will see a very large orange ball. This is your spirit energy growing in strength. When the

ball of energy is very large, stop rubbing your hands together.

   d. Watch the ball of energy rise above you and turn into a shower of sparks that rain down over you. As this happens, breathe the energy in and feel yourself getting stronger and full of energy.

   e. Open your eyes and enjoy the high energy you now have. The energy will be there for you when you quest. If need be, repeat the process.

3. Connect your spiritual life with your human life of now.

   a. Sit and relax. Breathe and feel your spirit energy. In your mind see a very safe place, a place with a path. Follow that path to a place where you can sit.

   b. Sit down on the side of the path where you can see left and right.

   c. Look down the path to the right and you will see a mist; from that mist will come a being. The being may be a color or a form of any kind. It may not look like a spirit because every spirit has its own form. This being is your spirit.

   d. Look to the left and you will see yourself as you are.

   e. These two will walk toward each other and they will meet, step into each other, and become one. As the two merge, your spiritual and human life join.

   f. Relax and breathe and open your eyes. Journal the event.

4. Meet your spirit guides.

Note: Meeting your spirit guides is a form of spiritual communion. You have a connection with a spirit who can help you see and learn in the Spirit World what your vision is about. It could be called channeling. I like to call it "having a talk with my guides and listening to the spiritual answers they share with me."

As with all channeling, this is not for everyone. If you have deep psychological problems—or find that the guides you connect with are negative or bring negative messages—please stop the communication. These connections are meant to bring light and information to your life and need to be done in the light. Your spirit guides are there to help you and give you a strong connection with Great Spirit and the Spirit World.

Are you here?

You are going to ask only "yes or no" questions. All questions can be asked once only.

Sit and close your eyes; after a while you will be able to connect with spirit guides with your eyes open. You may also find you connect with your guides in a sleep state.

When you connect to your spirit guide/s, you may have the physical sensation of pressure on the top of your head. This is the opening of the crown chakra. You may also feel a sensation on the left side of your body or face. This is the right side of the brain—the intuitive side—opening.

Listen to your thoughts.

Think, "Heya! Are you there?"

Relax and allow the answer to come naturally. You should hear a thought message with an affirmative answer.

Ask a string of "yes or no" questions that are not personal. You may stop and prepare them along the way. Spirit is there all the time to guide you. Get used to the idea of "listening" to simple messages.

A. Examples of questions for the spirits

❧ Why are you coming to me?

❧ What do you have to teach me?

❧ Where do I go in the Spirit World to see my vision?

❧ Who are you and why are you helping me on my vision quest?

❧ How do I use my vision?

❧ Where has my vision come from?

ò. With whom do I share my vision?

After talking to your guides, thank them and let them go on their way. Journal the questions you have asked and the answers given.

B. Getting to know your spirit guide

Again, use only "yes or no" questions—with one exception: find out the name of your main spirit guide.

This is a possible scenario:

ò. Greet your guide with whatever greeting you choose.

ò. Allow your thoughts to connect.

ò. Ask "can you answer" questions.

ò. After you ask each question, pause, listen to your thoughts, and connect with the answer.

ò. Then say: "I would like to know your name. Can you tell it to me please?"

ò. Wait for an affirmative answer. It should be immediate.

ò. If you have trouble getting the name—listen hard—then come as close to what you "hear" as you can. Spirit will accept whatever name you give.

ò. "Do you like the name _____?"

ò. Continue by asking more general questions.

ò. Journal the questions and the answers.

C. Talking to your guide about the All and the life of the guide

Prepare a set of "yes or no" questions pertaining to the All. Do not ask personal questions at this time.

Sample questions:

- How will your life be in the Spirit World?
- Is there life on other planets?
- Are there angels?
- Is there a dark side?
- What kingdom do you come from—animal, vegetable, mineral?

D. Talking to your guide about reality and other dimensions

- Are there many dimensions?
- Are there entities in those dimensions?
- Can a soul exist in more than one dimension?
- Does the future co-exist with the past and present?
- Do we have free will?
- Are you from the Creator?
- Do you do the will of the Creator?
- What are you here to do for me and my life?
- Do you have messages for me?

E. Getting personal

By now you should be feeling comfortable with your guide. So this is the time to start with some personal spiritual questions. Do not ask about your romantic life or job! Basically ask "yes or no" questions.

Some easy questions may be asked that require explanation.

- Are you my only spirit guide?
- How many do I have?
- What is your function in my life?
- Am I on the right spiritual path?
- Will you guide me to the next part of my spirit journey?
- Do I pray enough?

🙡 Will you lead me to a book or website to learn what I need to know?

🙡 Is my current teacher okay? (if you have one) Or is it time to move on?

🙡 Do I need to move to a new location to find my destiny? If the answer is yes—it is up to you to start naming places. Still ask only "yes or no" answers.

Continue questions. Take notes. *Do not* ask for long, detailed explanations.

It might be fun to ask a question of each guide to see if you can tell the difference in their frequency, thus getting more familiar with them. Address your guides by name. This takes practice for some people. For those who have been listening to their guides for years without realizing that they were connecting with spirit, this will be easy.

F. Speaking with your guide about your family

🙡 Do I have a strong spiritual connection with my family?

🙡 From whom in my family do I get the strongest spiritual support?

🙡 Are there people in my family I need to get closer to?

🙡 Are there people in my family I should forgive?

🙡 Is it time for me to start a family of my own?

G. Your career/job

Continue with "yes or no" questions. The workplace can have many emotional issues attached to it. Perhaps prepare a list of questions for the day. Still keep things easy and direct.

Begin with a greeting to your guides. You can tell your guides that you are here today to discuss your job or career, but in all probability they already know that.

Sample questions:

- 🙣 Is the career I have chosen a lifetime career?
- 🙣 Will I have various changes of career in this lifetime?
- 🙣 Should I go to school and train for a career?
- 🙣 Do I need formal education or training for my career?
- 🙣 Am I best suited to be a _____? (Create a list of desired job choices.)
- 🙣 Businesses: would I do better alone?
- 🙣 With one partner?
- 🙣 Two partners?
- 🙣 Can I trust _____?
- 🙣 Will my business merge? Evolve into something else? Fail?
- 🙣 Is my job a dead end?
- 🙣 Does my boss appreciate my work?
- 🙣 Do I have personal conflict in the office?
- 🙣 Will my race/ethnic background, etc., impede my chances of finding a career I love or of moving upward in my career?
- 🙣 Am I settling for less than I could be because I am lazy?
- 🙣 Am I smarter than I realize?
- 🙣 Could I return to school after years of absence?
- 🙣 Can I find a career that I am passionate about?
- 🙣 Will I stay at this job until I retire?
- 🙣 Can I work from home? With my computer?

You will think of dozens of questions.

H. Your love life

You are finally ready to ask "yes or no" questions about your love life. Remember first answers count!

Sample questions if you have a partner now:

- 🙣 Is _____ my soul mate?

- Is _____ my lifetime partner or will I have another?
- Is my partner growing spiritually as I am?
- Is this important to keeping us together?
- Have we grown apart?
- Am I holding onto a relationship that is over?
- Does _____ really love me?
- Can _____ love in a spiritual way?
- Does my low self-esteem enter the picture?
- Why do I stay with _____?

Sample questions if you do not have a partner now:
- Does my soul mate exist on the Earth plane now—in a physical body?
- Is my soul mate my spirit guide?
- Will I marry? Live with someone?
- Do I need therapy to maintain a relationship?
- Will I ever have a child? (if childless)
- Is a lifetime-commitment partner what I really want—or would I prefer to change partners as my needs and theirs change?
- Would my soul's needs best be met by living alone? With a mate?
- Is my destiny on Earth other than marriage and children?
- Do I have a soul mate out there? Describe him/her to me—physical description, age, career, where the person lives.
- How will we meet? Social occasion? Chance meeting? Other?
- Will that person be ready for a full-time commitment? If not, why not?
- I have just met _____. Is this my true soul mate? Ask detailed questions.

I. Your goals in life
It's time for "yes or no" questions about your goals in life. By now

you should sense that your guide is near you and ready to answer your questions. Greet him/her in whatever way you choose.

Sample questions:
- Are my goals in life realistic?
- Should the allow myself "the sky's the limit" when creating my goals?
- Do I need to change my goals pertaining to my love life? marriage? work? other?
- Will I ever realize my goals?

Think of other questions.

5. See your vision.

After you have balanced your energy and are ready to vision quest, go into your vision area and stay for at least 24 hours. Do not leave the area. Four days are the best and fullest connection for a vision. Any amount of time you decide upon is all right, as long as the vision has come.

Journal your vision and draw a sketch of the vision to study from.

· 2 ·

Choices Within the Quest

I hear the drum beating and walk to the door. There at the fire circle are the staff, seven dedicated students who walk with the wholeness of their vision, knowing themselves in spirit and physicality. They are ready to work with the four chosen students. Drumming on their hand-drums softly, they are watching the flames dance in the night sky.

"It is time." I gather the students to make choices about the vision quest. "Tonight I will explain the medicine bundle and you will hear stories of students who have quested. The adventure of the quest has been chosen. It is a wilderness retreat. We will be leaving in two weeks."

The students have a lot of work to do. I look over my students' information sheets and see that they will be questing to find answers to questions about feeling angry and lost, about obsessive drinking and drug use, and about feelings of pain, loss, and emptiness. They seek answers to questions about life, such as why we are human beings. These four students have experienced divorce, debt, molestation, rape, emptiness, loneliness, fear, and failure.

The choices within the quest are not easy. They need to choose to face themselves and their fears.

I am ready to speak. I step into the circle. The drumming becomes very soft and Pepper Dog ends it with four final beats.

I look at the students and ask, "Are you sure that a vision quest is your choice? Are you sure that you wish to embark upon something that is all mental but may involve great physical hardships?"

They look back at me—John, Cathy, Lee, and Linda—excitement in their eyes.

Cathy says, "It is my choice and I want to vision quest. I've heard that you're a good teacher and you will share your magical healing with us."

"Magical healing is the way of native truths," I say. "They are the ways of my mother, who led me to my vision quest and showed me the Rainbow Medicine Path. She allowed me to see that each student who comes before Grandmother/Grandfather/Great Spirit is gifted with the memory of their life in spirit. You have a lot of work to do. You have your vision bundle to build, your prayer sticks to make. You have your vision square to bring together. I will pass out instructions for making these things and a list of items to go into your medicine bundle, so that you can make sure you have with you what you need to go on a vision quest."

ITEMS FOR THE VISION QUEST MEDICINE BUNDLE

Your medicine bundle can be a homemade skin pouch or a bag, or it can be a flat pie   ce of cloth you place objects in and roll into a bundle. The medicine bundle holds the items below, as well as your blanket, herbs, prayer sticks, feathers, rocks, and any other items you use during vision quest and other sacred ceremonies.

1. appropriate clothing to fit the climate and the environment
2. rainproof gear or a waterproof jacket
3. toothbrush, toothpaste, and a small glass for rinsing out your mouth
4. a sleeping bag and mat, a pillow, and a ground sheet (a rain tarp)
5. a flashlight
6. sunscreen
7. a hat
8. sunglasses
9. natural insect repellent
10. a journal and a few pens
11. toilet paper
12. a small shovel
13. a paper bag
14. large water container, water
15. a bare minimum of food and keep it to hiking food: trail mix and other easily digestible food, unless you need to depart from this for medical reasons
16. duct tape
17. backpack
18. whistle
19. nylon cord

20. 4 vision poles and a bag to carry them
21. 4 vision cords
22. 4 flags that go with your vision equipment
23. waterproof matches
24. medicine blanket

"Traditionally, quests are done without food, unless you need to eat for medical reasons, such as diabetes or hypoglycemia. You might try doing your vision quest with very little or no food. This is why I recommend high protein and high carbohydrate trail mixes and dried fruit. Personal power doesn't come from your decision about eating; it comes from making a commitment and abiding by it with no regrets. It's very important that you do not become fatigued from not eating. Food that comes with you should provide a lot of energy and it should be as fresh as possible. You want dried food. Dried nuts and dried meat are good sources of protein, and you'll have no spoilage. I do not allow drinking of any type of liquor or the taking of any type of medicine, unless your doctor has prescribed it.

"Each of you is responsible for digging your own latrine and placing your waste under cover. The brown paper bag is for your toilet paper and is to be disposed of at the lodge trash dumpster.

"You will need a personal medicine blanket—a blanket that you choose to use while you are visioning to cover yourself and protect your spirit—to keep you warm in the physical world and safe in the spiritual world.

"You will need good hiking shoes. No cameras will be allowed, no music, nor any electronic instruments or electrical appliances. There will be no electricity. I suggest you bring some waterproof matches and make sure you have an extra pen or two in case you run out of ink."

I see that the students are taking notes furiously.

Cathy looks up and says, "It's wonderful that you have this organized. I feel very safe in this camp and I love the people who are sitting here with me." She glances around the circle and the staff members nod their heads.

"A strong bond is beginning to form within the circle," I think. "It's always a wonderful thing to watch people seek out their wholeness and call upon the spiritual guidance of a vision quest to do so."

SEVEN SPIRIT WORDS FOR VISION QUESTING

The yellow staff member, Butterfly Sky, stands and begins to speak.

"Each of you has come to embark upon ancient rites of passage to gain knowledge of the inner self. I would like to present to you the words that will be your guides within your vision quest. What you do comes from the vision of Wolf Moondance—the sun, moon, and seven stars—for which we are grateful. Her vision was given to her through the teachings of her mother, and we honor Marie Screaming Eagle. Though she is no longer with us in the physical world, she helps us from the Spirit World.

"Seven spirit words will guide you along the way in your journey. The first word is red and it is 'seek' or 'seeking.' This word will guide you in finding your own spirit.

"The next word is orange and it is 'connecting.' This is the work that you will be doing with your physical understanding of the spiritual meanings of the symbols and visions from your vision.

"The third word, the yellow word, is 'crying.' This is an old vision word, which means the calling forth of your animal totems and guides.

"Your fourth word—the green word—is 'reaching.' This word connects you to the medicine wheel word 'growth.' You will open your heart and walk toward the magical healing that will take place in your everyday consciousness, as well as in the actions in your life.

"The fifth word, your blue word, is 'feel.' Feel is the doorway to understanding, which is your purpose in vision questing—understanding why things have happened and will happen, and you will be guided through your feelings in the future.

"Your sixth, your purple word, is 'ancient knowledge.' As you call upon your spirit, you will be looking at wisdom from the Spirit World.

"As you walk forward, you will come to your burgundy word, which is 'wholeness.' When you achieve wholeness, you are in balance, you are full of success, your energies are used in a good way, and I promise you will have inner peace and tranquility for the rest of your human life. Thank you very much for listening."

Butterfly Sky gently sits down.

I look at the students and see that they're taking good notes. They're still writing.

"I see that you're eager to learn. This is a good thing. When you're on the Good Red Road, you are walking with the truth of Great Spirit. Lee, can you speak to why you have chosen to do vision quest?"

He looks up and brushes his black hair out of his deep dark eyes. "Yes, I can speak to this very clearly. I am looking to discover my life's purpose. It is very important to me that I not waste my physical existence. I know that there is a mystery that mankind is a part of, and I choose to find the very core of my existence and connect to the Great Mystery. When I was growing up I was in a lot of pain and there was no one to help. I was told by an aunt to pray to God for help and everything would be okay. Well, I did and nothing changed. I wanted to have God in my life, but there was never an answer, and the pain and abuse didn't stop 'til I ran away and became my own person. I used drugs, thinking I could find an answer through them. No answer—only drug problems. I was told by a student of yours that I can see in the spirit and that I will understand the vision I will get. I want to find the spiritual path I see with all my heart. I want it to be real." He folds his hands and sits quietly waiting for me to answer.

"I find that this is the real purpose for most people: they are looking to discover their purpose. When we go out to vision quest, we want to break free from the limited beliefs we have about ourselves. We call for a vision to be able to hear the voice of Great Spirit. As we open our minds to Great Spirit, we are told our goals and answers in life. A lot of the time, we find the answers are simple. We find that we are to live on a spirit path and have life goals, and understand that other people are lost, angry, and out of control, and they influence our lives. What does that mean to you, Linda?"

Linda's sweet round face and soft brown eyes touch my heart as she begins to speak clearly.

"It means that I choose to step into the sacred circle and connect with Great Spirit. I want to harness the powers that are given to me and that will allow me to see deep within myself. It's a chance to understand that I'm number one in my life. That I have to set the goals of my life from the will of Great Spirit, and through the vision, I will find my path, which is truth for me."

"I like your answer, Linda. You will find that to do that, you must comfort and free yourself from every fear you have. You've just begun the tremendous amount of emotional work that it takes to heal the wounds."

Cathy nods. Her hair, pulled back in a ponytail, is dark chocolate brown, and in it she has tied beautiful black feathers.

"I want to develop my inner peace. I want to know peace of mind. It is my desire, more than anything, to walk away from the feeling of being lost and to let go of the things that haunt me deep into the night. You see, I was raised that we pray and all the answers come. We were taught in my home that to talk to the spirits is bad, 'cause we don't know which spirits will get us and 'cause death and sickness.

So I have a lot of fear and I want to live in peace and harmony with the Spirit World," she says.

"Those are good reasons. You are coming here, seeking, wishing to connect, crying for a vision, reaching to feel the deep ancient knowledge that will bring wholeness to your existence. The most important thing when working with a vision is not to be scared of the spirits who teach and listen to your thoughts.

"You are your own leader when you vision quest. Only you can talk the words of the vision, only you can walk the vision.

"We will be questing for seven days, three of those days will be for teaching and prayer work and four of those days will be intense personal vision work. While you are working you will wear the same clothes, no bathing or grooming will go on. You will have time for that at the end of your quest.

"The rest of the time, we will be sharing and working on tools that are needed to do ceremony. You have learned a lot, and as you walk forward, you will learn a lot more. The vision quest that you go upon is a personal quest. It is up to you to reach within yourself, dig deep within your pain and come to a place where you're in balance. Do you have any questions that we might be able to help with?" I ask.

John says, "What exactly do I do on my quest? I know that there will be ceremony, but how do I put into context exactly what I do?"

I look at him and his crystal blue eyes twinkle.

"John, see if you can tell me yourself."

He sits there for a few moments and then says, " I wrote down a few things I'd like to do. I want to cry, I want to let go, I want to forgive, and I want to heal. Right?"

What a gentle spirit he is, I think. "Yes that is a good answer." I go on, "That will happen. You will watch the nature around you and look for symbols and actions among the animals and the others that watch. It's important that you breathe, and most of all that you work in your journal.

"It's a time to sleep and think. It's a time to pray, to open your mind and listen to the spirit words."

Lee asks, "What if I don't get any vision? Will I have failed?"

"There are many things that a vision quest does for you. Failing is not one of them. You don't always see the picture right off, or the symbol," I say. "A vision quest is a powerful inner journey and sometimes it takes time to understand what you've felt or seen. You might have seen a bee fly past you and that's all you had. The bee might be interpreted as hard work and a need to get busy. Maybe you aren't ready for the vision, is the answer. Maybe the vision is going to speak to you in days to come. The answer that I can give you is that no one fails at a vision quest. It can seem that way—because the rest of the world is black and white, and it may look as if you have failed if you have not seen a picture in your mind. I must say, though, that there can be no real failing, for failure is opportunity, and the vision quest brings the opportunity for you to put more work into your vision. Wait for the vision to speak to you in days ahead, in dreamtime, or even all of a sudden—when it will just come to you."

The students listen carefully as we cover questions like, is it normal not to eat in vision.

"It is very important that you eat, and the way I teach vision quest, you have a choice. I feel very strongly that you will obtain your vision and your food will not take anything away from what you are trying to do. There are quests in which food is taken away. I feel that that is harsh. If you limit your food, you will be okay. Medical problems need to be treated in a gentle way and with an understanding of what the doctor has required of you."

STUDENTS' QUESTIONS ABOUT THE VISION QUEST

The students had many more questions about the vision quest.

Q. **What do I do if a wild animal approaches and tries to hurt me?**

A. We have a rough time when we are in a vision quest knowing if the animal we see is real or a spirit animal. The staff will be posted close to you and will hear you if you cry out for help. If it is real, they will journal the animal and make it leave.

You need to pay very close attention to the animal and journal it. Work with confidence and know you are walking the path of the spirit of the animal. You need the answers from the animal as part of the understanding of your vision, physical or spiritual, for it is teaching the meanings of the physical and the spiritual reason you are seeing it.

Q. **What do I do if I have to leave the circle to go to the bath room?**

A. You can leave your square or use your shovel and stay in the square; just make sure you keep up with what you see and feel and hear. And journal all of it.

Q. **If it rains, should I quit?**

A. No, rain is a part of the vision you are working with. Balance and look at the reason you don't want to be wet. Journal all your feelings and then you can work with them. Know that the rain is a clearing and cleansing spirit. Know that it is a very powerful spirit from the West. It speaks of the physical and the cycles of life and a need to clear and clean.

Q. If I get cold, should I stop?

A. Cold is to be worked with, as it is from the North and speaks of the wolf. It is leading you to the mind—the strong mind. Know the truth and know that you are facing death and the fear of death. Warm yourself, wrap up in your medicine blan ket, and look at your fears and the short time we are humankind. Look to the spirit of the self.

Q. If I'm scared, have I caused my vision quest to fall apart?

A. How could you do that? Fear is to be faced. You will only fall apart if you run or walk away from the vision square. Stay there and face the power of the vision and all the guides who come to you. Remember your vision is to line out goals and paths to a good and strong physical life—a life with all in balance. The spirits want to guide and bless you—not scare you.

Q. If my mind drifts and I can only think of personal matters, should I stop my vision quest?

A. That is the first thing that happens, and it happens a lot. As humans, we want to avoid our vision because we are full of fear. Or maybe we don't really want to know the truth; we just want to keep on the path we are on. Journal all fears and anger and sadness you feel and turn to your vision for strength and purpose. Study the vision and find the knowledge it holds. This will bring understanding to you when you worry or fear.

Q. What if I don't understand what I've seen or heard?

A. You don't, at first. That is the work of the vision. You study and learn the meanings of the colors, flowers, stones, herbs, dreams, and symbols—all the things in your vision. If you don't understand, there is vision study. You seek a shaman, a visionary teacher, or go back out to work with the self and the vision.

These are ways to handle it. It will take time, as it is the study of a lifetime, a way of living—not a quick fix.

Q. What if I can't see the spiritual part of myself?
A. It is East, as I teach in my book Rainbow Medicine.

Take the following steps to see the spirit self.

1. See a path in your mind, a place that is known and safe to you. Walk down the path until you find a pond.
2. Walk to the pond and look into it. You will see a reflection, your spirit self.
3. Journal what you see.
4. Just let your mind see, don't try to understand or change or make it the way you want. Take it as it is.
5. Journal everything you see, for all is you.
6. Understand that seeing is also hearing, feeling, and knowing. Often it feels made up, but everything we do and know is taught or made up. Let go and understand the spirit side of the self.
7. When you have a spiritual answer it feels right; you feel a knowing that you are doing good and all is well.

If you like being a horse, then you are one, and the horse will help open the door to your understanding of the spiritual self.

Q. What if I don't understand the voice or the sightings of Creator?
A. It will be fear that keeps you from understanding. Journal your fear and then ask why. Answer and work with your needs and-wants. Are you feeling child-like and as if you need someone else to answer the questions? If so, grow—and answer the-

questions for yourself. Know that all is Creator and you will have all you need and want. Don't be fearful or worried—feel the joy of knowing and seeing.

"All of these questions and many more will be answered as we go along," I tell them. "Each one of you has asked good questions and you have strong feelings. Remember that you are crying for a vision. You are reaching for the opportunity to realize and understand. I would like you to take time and work with your questions. Open your spirit journal and start working."

John looks at me questioningly. "I can't see how I'm going to understand any of this."

"It is very important to listen," Dancing Spirit, the staff member in purple, says. "You can write, or talk on a tape recorder, but each thought and each feeling and each thing you see and come to understand needs to be recorded while you are in your vision time. Because everything plays a part in the story that you're seeking. Vision questing is tapping into old spiritual wisdom as well as projecting your path through the wisdom that you obtain. Take notes about everything you think and feel. Take notes about the first thing you see in the morning and the last thing you see at night. Everything that you encounter needs to be interpreted and understood. Ancient wisdom is the complexity of the dirt, the simplicity of a water drop. It is important to journal everything. Do you see what I mean, John?"

"Yes, I can understand that. So, it's things that we dream, things that we hear, things that we feel, things that we see?" John said with a smile.

"Absolutely," I say, "for everything we do in the vision quest has a meaning, and it doesn't all happen in one week. It doesn't even happen in a year, or several. My vision unrolls every day by allowing me to hear more and more of the ancient wisdom. The choices within the quest tell the spiritual story of the whole self. The vision shows you your totem and guides. It shows you your spirit color and gives you the teachings of your spiritual path. You draw from your vision the knowing of yourself and the strength to live life without crutches and false teachings. You know the self and you make that personal to you.

"Look into the fire and you'll see. You'll see the power of the vision quest. It takes your wanting to see and know what the vision looks like. It will appear as a picture, clear to you. It may also feel like a knowing—like two flowers by a creek. You see this vision and feel peace. You know from the vision that you must have a creek (flow) in your life and want to live with the flow of the spirit, which is what the creek symbolizes. Your vision will talk to your mind and you will find and know the answers of the vision."

Aho.

FURTHER QUESTIONS ABOUT THE VISION QUEST

Q. How much time is involved with a vision quest?

A. The greatest amount of time is involved in preparation. It takes time to gather your supplies and tools. Many different times can be involved for visioning—an hour, a day, a weekend, a four-day, seven-day, or 21-day vision quest. Remember that the quest really goes on for the rest of your life—journaling and understanding and interpreting your vision.

Q. How do I control my fear when I am on a vision quest?

A. Ask yourself first what you are afraid of. Also, realize it is okay to have fear; it is a normal emotion. Ask yourself if your fear is a physical matter that you need to stop your vision quest to deal with. Understand that you're coming to vision to get over your fear. Realize that you will be doing a ceremony to dismiss and balance your fear, so you can recognize that your fears are brought on by lack of knowledge or understanding.

Q. How can I go on a vision quest if I am on prescription medication or under the care of a doctor?

A. It is important that your doctor understand that you're going on a vision quest. It is essential that you have someone with you to help you if you should become ill. A retreat vision quest is a good way to vision, because you will have people around to make sure you're okay. Continue taking your prescription med ication and make no changes from what the doctor has told you.

Q. Do I have to be Native American to have a vision quest?

A. Vision quests are open to everyone. It is the will of Great Spirit for you to understand the direction you are to take in your existence. It has always been a Native American teaching, but vision quests are open to and taught by all races.

Q. Is Great Spirit the same as God? Is the vision quest a Christian activity?

A. Great Spirit is all—God is all. All things that are good are Great Spirit and vision questing is good. The actual religion of vision quest is none. If other teachers choose to say that a vision quest comes from a certain religion, that is their philos- ophy. In this lodge, through my teachings, a vision quest is an open magical healing for all people who seek it. The Native American part of the vision quest is in encountering the four directions. You are in the medicine wheel, connected to nature and the teachings of Great Spirit, which are carried on by teachers of Native American teachings (in this case, the teaching my mother passed to me). Each vision quest is unique to its own tribe, nation, or quest guide and teacher.

Q. **How will I know how to build my vision square?**
A. You will be instructed how to obtain four direction poles and the vision cords that go with the poles. You will use shamanic journey to understand the purpose of your vision square and achieve your vision. Also, look at the instructions for building a vision square in this book.

Q. **What if I can't see in the spiritual sense?**
A. Great Spirit never forsakes anyone. When you are called to a vision, the vision is granted. When you are seeing in the spiritual sense, sometimes it feels like things are very easy and they should be difficult. Sometimes, things are animated and humorous. As time passes, you will understand the sense of the vision you have obtained. It's not unusual to think that you don't see. As you work with your vision and come to an understanding, you'll know if you've had a vision or not. It's easy to see in the spiritual sense. It's hard to believe in what you've seen.

Q. **How many times do you go on a vision quest?**
A. You go on a vision quest 'til you have a vision. Then you can go out to sit with the vision and listen and think about the truth and voice of the vision. Listen to your thoughts and the knowledge you have learned from your vision. Your vision can have other thoughts added to it, but the original vision is the main one, and it may add to itself to teach you things that are important in your daily life.

You can sit with your vision yearly, monthly, weekly, or daily to look and listen to your thoughts and the learning of the vision. You can go on a vision quest to receive more information from your vision, but the first time you receive your vision it will be very clear to you. From then on it is talking to the vision and receiving more knowledge from the vision.

Q. Do you have to be of a certain belief to have a vision or go on a vision quest?

A. There is no belief that cannot go on a vision quest. The vision quest is often thought of as Native American, but all faiths are able to communicate with Great Spirit/Creator/God. What is needed to have a vision is a calling or a desire to have a vision.

Q. Is a vision quest the same as meditation?

A. No, meditation is a relaxing mode, and a vision is a spiritual journey where you connect with your spirit guides and Spirit World teachings. You can start a vision, though, in a meditative state.

Q. Do you have several visions in your life?

A. When you go out on a vision quest, you are looking for guidance. The vision you receive is your personal guide through life. You can have many small visions that are connected to the main vision. A vision is not a daydream or a night dream, even though you can connect to your life vision through a daydream or night dream.

Q. If you are a Christian, does going on a vision quest change your belief and separate you from the church?

A. No, it will bring you closer to Creator/God. You will be open to the holy spirit and hear and see the message of God more clearly. Christ went out in the dessert and had a vision of temptation and it helped him with the choice to serve God's will.

Q. Is it just as good to do a vision quest at home? Or is it better to go out in the wilderness?

A. It is best if you can go outdoors. You have a stronger connection to spirit outdoors. Also you are in a different environment than your safe home. You're in a place where you disconnect from all you know and are open to the spirits. You are where you can see wild life and make spiritual connections with the earth mother and all she wants to say to you. If you have to do the quest indoors, be sure that you will not be disturbed. You make the vision square as described in the book, except you use the cord on the floor and tie the colors onto the cord. You must be alone and uninterrupted for the period you choose to vision. No phones are to be answered; it is best to unplug them. No pets—best to place them in the care of another. You cannot leave the square except for bathroom breaks, but take no shower or bath until the vision time is over. Follow the solo vision instructions in the book and do all the work in each chapter.

Q. When I am doing a solo vision quest, do I need someone to tell me what my vision means or can I decode it all myself?

A. A vision is very private. It is best to find understanding for yourself. If you need help, use books that have teachings in them or the computer, if you do not have a medicine person, shaman, or visionary to help. That away you can let the spirit guide you to what is truth in your vision. Keep what works for you and let the rest go.

Q. What if I have fears of evil and feel something evil will become attached to me if I go on a vision quest?

A. Evil is a state of thinking that opens up fears and throws you off balance. Stick to your truth and have confidence.

Remember that fear comes from control. No evil can come to you if you do not call for it. I would be careful not to let the teachings of others slip into your mind. If you walk to your vision with thoughts of light and good, the spirits will watch over truth and goodness will be the outcome. Do not carry fear, guilt, and worry into the vision quest. You need to clear your mind of fears, angers and pain. The vision has come to help your daily life and you need to unblock your mind. As you clear your mind for the vision, it will help you heal in all ways.

Q. Can you have vision quests with mixed genders?

A. Yes, you can, or you can set up men's and women's quests. The choice is up to the quest leader and also what you feel you want to do. A vision quest does not have to be same gender, nor does it have to be mixed gender.

Q. What happens in a youth vision quest?

A. The vision quest is the same for all ages. With a youth quest the young ones are set up to vision in age groups: 4–9 years old; 10–21 years. We place more staff on duty with the young ones.

Q. What do I do with the vision I receive? How do I keep it so I will remember?

A. Your vision should be drawn on a paper or an animal skin so it becomes a bundle. After you draw the vision to the best of your ability, roll it up and cover it with red cloth, closed on both ends and tied with cord. Then place it under your bed or on your personal altar at home and open it as needed.

Q. Should I tell others about my vision?

A. If you feel they need to know, if you understand your vision and feel it is to be shared. Don't talk of the vision because you think you should or because it's cool. Use the vision as you need to follow the will of Creator. Follow the thought, picture it in your mind. Keep the vision as you have seen it. Never change the vision because someone tells you to.

Q. In a marriage, is it good for one person to have a vision and the other not to have one?

A. It can be fine and it can cause trouble. When you have a spouse who cares about you and your knowledge, it is good. When your spouse feels left out, you need to help the spouse turn inward and start the path of the vision quest for him- or herself.

THE VISION QUEST TEST

This test is about your reason for questing. There are four questions; pick one and then read the explanation to determine your questing personality.

1. Are you open to mystery and do you love to seek the unknown?
2. Are you always wondering and looking to tomorrow?
3. Do you have a strong connection to nature, the Earth, and all living things of the wilderness?
4. Do you want to rid yourself of past pain and the pains of today that you feel are your failures?

If you selected question

1: You are a person of confidence and strength. Your path on the vision quest is that of the seeker. You will nurture yourself and achieve your vision.

2: Your life is one of growth and change. Your path is beauty and your vision is fresh and waiting for you to claim it.

3: You are balanced and make good choices. Your vision will bring much success to your life and raise and enrich your energy.

4: You reach for the trail of truth, and healing will be the beginning of your vision quest. As you travel on, you will see your purpose and you will have inner peace as proof.

If you chose #1, tie a red cloth around your leg above the knee for the week of your vision quest. Cut the cloth 2 inches (5cm) wide and 36 inches (1m) long. Wear your red cloth while you are on your vision quest.

If you chose #2, wear a green cloth cut to the same size and tied above your knee.

If you chose #3, your cloth is orange.

If you chose #4, your cloth is blue.

Wear the cloth, whatever the color, all the while you are on your vision quest. These cloths remind you that you are sacred, that you have passed the test of your vision quest, and that you will know what your vision has to offer to your life. Keep this cloth to wear when you sit in prayer about your vision. The cloth has vision powers, and especially when you feel weak or sick, it will give you the strength to stay on the vision path. Place it with your sacred objects at your altar or in a safe place.

Aho.

· 3 ·

The Sacred Vision Site

"I come to the mountain. I hear many songs. I can see. I want to know and walk away from the pain. I look at the road I must travel. The journey is steep and hard. As I make the climb, I realize that I know the purpose of my vision. Everything in life is hard. I make it that way. As I climb to the base camp, I have begun to see the rough road I have walked. I see the hawk pass. I hear the raven. Their life is easy and their flight is of peace. This is the path I choose, the one of peace."

—Linda

Linda is 32 and a housewife from Houston, Texas. She was raised in a Christian home where you did not ask spiritual questions. Linda suffered at the hands of an uncle; she was raped by him at the age of 12. Her family did not believe her when she told them.

Full of wonder, Linda saw spirits at the age of seven and no one would talk about it with her or help. She was often told she was full of the devil. She knew what she saw was the truth, but it was hard to get anyone to listen to her about anything. She was pushed through her childhood and never taken seriously. She started drinking at 18 to calm the pain, and she kept her drinking problem secret. She came for vision quest to learn and to be spiritual, to answer the questions of childhood, and to overcome the pain of the rape. She had heard from someone who had experienced a vision quest that spiritual healing is very powerful.

It is evening and the fire is crackling. I hear the voices of the stars. "Good evening," I tell the circle of students. "If you hand in your homework, I'll check it over in a little bit and pass it back out. At this point, you're beginning to understand that you are taking a life-altering journey. The vision quest clears your mind. It helps you to open to the deepest voice of your spirit and it shows you the simple ways."

The students have the glow of the spirit around them. I hold my black hat gently in my hands and look around the circle. I feel the fatigue and the excitement of the students. "We have a short time left and a lot to prepare. Tonight, we are going to take a shamanic journey to your vision site.

"This is a location that you will seek out once we get to base camp. You will be going high into the mountains, and you will find a place that will look similar to what you see now. Shamanic journey is easy; it is a journey that you take in your mind's eye into the spirit, where you will connect with your vision."

The students prepare themselves, as do the staff members, and become quiet and relaxed. Two of the staff start a soft drumming, a gentle beat, one that connects us to the heartbeat of Earth. We take a deep breath in and out and continue breathing four times. We relax.

"Before each one of you, a familiar path is winding its way around the mountain. You may begin to look for a place that you would like to stay, a place where you want to set your vision square. There you will interact with the spirits. Notice everything around you. Are you high up? Do you have a view? Are you at peace? Are you beneath the trees? What do you see? Walk around in your journey and find a comfortable place that you will seek out in this physical world that matches the one you see in your spirit."

The students continue breathing in and out and the drumming goes on.

I look to the center of the room at the circle of seven colors. I see the seeker calling the ancient wisdom. I see the students walking around seeking out their places. I see our base camp with a pole and the burgundy flag swaying gently in the breeze. The pieces of cloth tied on the pole wave us home. The drumming comes to a halt, and in a minute people start opening their eyes.

"Have you seen what you're looking for?" I ask the students. They nod yes and smile.

"That was a lot easier than I thought it was going to be. It was a wonderful place," Linda speaks. She has a twinkle in her eyes and a peaceful feeling in her voice.

"Yep, that was my place," Lee says. "I went to the spot where the small creek rushes by."

Cathy and John also speak of their places, and the staff shares what they felt before they took their journeys.

"Will we find those exact spots?" Lee asks.

"It is very possible," I reply. "You will come to a place that is very much like what you saw."

"Will we go and look some more?" Cathy asks.

"No, I think it's best that we journal what we know."

The students begin to write down what they have seen. The drummer drums softly as one of the staff lights the sage and sweetgrass and fans it with beautiful speckled feathers. The smoke is sent around to bless each person and to cleanse any fears or worries that might be in the room.

I notice that Cathy has a strange look on her face, and I say, "What is it?"

She says, "What was the black object that was standing by my rock? It was tall—it was a being. It was waiting. It was something I see almost every night when I go to sleep. It feels as if it wants to steal my breath."

"I hear you—I feel this is your inner fear, and that is one of the things we must face as we go to vision. The spirit is a part of you, a part you will balance and replace with wisdom."

John nods and says, "That's nothing like what I saw darting around. These things darted over here and they darted over there and then they went beneath a rock and waited. They said they'd see me there. What does that mean?" he asked.

Several staff members look at each other and drop their heads. Pepper Dog says, "Our inner fears and pain run and hide. They try to make us forget, and then they come back attacking later—scaring us with old memories. Your vision gives you a clear and clean feeling. You can get past the hiding ones."

"I don't like what you're saying," Linda says. "It's beginning to worry me. It's making me frightened. I don't want to encounter something that's dark and negative. I've come to my vision quest to do away with those feelings."

The thoughts run fast in my mind. "You can't always control what goes on. You don't always have the power. It's best we move on and speak of the visions that we're going to take. Stay with the choice of vision, look forward and know you have your fears on the run. They are spirit and the vision heals them. This will be a strong healing and very magical."

The candles flicker and silence falls across the room. You can hear the heartbeats. It's always like this when it's time to make our commitments.

"It is our personal need to encounter our fears. Some people like to call them their demons. Some people call them their monsters. When we have to confront our worries and anxieties, our fears and emotional disturbances, it's better just to call them what they are—our fear."

"I've always had fear," Lee says. "That's one of my main reasons for wanting to go on a vision quest. I want to have the inner strength to stand alone and not be scared. I think it's something that humans just can't control. I don't think we learn to handle our fears in the right way when we are little. Anyway, I didn't."

I take a deep breath and let it out, thinking that it isn't always the way it seems. It isn't easy, young ones. Sometimes when we encounter our monsters, we are facing the very thing that destroys us—our childhood pain, rape, jail, not being believed. We will find answers within our vision, for it is the voice and knowing from the Spirit World, from Creator.

"What are you thinking, Wolf?" Cathy asks. "Your face has become old."

"Oh, it's just part of a vision and it will soon pass. This is not the night to worry. This is the night to understand that we seek the sacred circle of vision, that we are going to our camp where we will place our personal vision square and embark upon our totality."

"I don't like the dark," Cathy says. "Dark is not something I can do. We will be camping where there's light, won't we?"

Several of the staff members snicker, turn their heads and drop their eyes.

Jack Red Fox, the one in red, speaks. "There will be no light. It will be mostly dark, or mostly daylight, and even when you're in the light, it will seem dark. There will be confusion; there will be emptiness and everything you face will be worse than you see. Now how about that? Are you ready to go or stop? It's seeking that you've chosen. But will you confront your small, anxious worries and fears, and acts of imbalance—or give up? Are you in this vision quest to become whole and understand your totality, or not?"

The four students look at each other.

"It isn't facing something scary that bothers me," John said. "It's the lack of understanding. I have fear and pain. I don't know if I'll be able to see a vision and if I don't, then what?"

"Wait!" says White Mouse, the staff member in orange. "It is not yours to know. It's yours to trust. When you walk to your vision quest, you must encounter the forest, the wisdom of the woods, and the spirits that come to teach you. You must stand with the things you don't know in order to realize that they cannot harm you. Balance is what you seek, connection is what you need, and nothing else will do you any good. You can walk out, or you can walk forward."

The students are silent. I sit watching them, wondering which one will give up first. We humankind often come to vision because we hear someone say their vision worked for them. Or we come for a vision because we've read about it and want to experience it.

"You know," I say, "we have a ways to go, and turning back is always a possibility, but when you quit your vision, you'll be where you are now; you could even be worse, for you could feel like a failure. You could have feelings of being a quitter. You could feel the weaknesses that mar your personality. To vision quest, you must allow the magic to happen."

"Let me speak of an experience," says Cat Eyes, the staff member in green. "When you are reaching, you are climbing. Spirituality is not a level experience. It is not an ordinary daily pace. It is not physicality. It is the place where you're never prepared. It is the place where lessons come from. The ancient ones speak of the trials and tribulations that a human faces. You have come here to study with the Wolf, to follow the path to your vision quest. There's nothing easy about walking off into the woods. You will gather together and be carried in vans. You will take an extensive trip and at some point, you will be blindfolded. The reason for the blindfold is so you will leave your physical existence and enter into the spirit realms. The blindfold is the symbol of leaving and entering. You are reaching beyond your physicality. To understand your human emotions, acceptance is the best medicine to walk in. It is the one where you understand that your questing is standing in the presence of your intentions—that you understand why you want to step out. You will get wet and you will get cold. You will get tired, you will get frustrated, and you will want to quit. If your spirit guides grace you, then you will have some-one to hold your hand when times are empty and lonely. Reaching is going beyond. You have been called to your vision, which you know.

"I came to a place where I realized I had no control over what I called my human life. At any time during this experience, you can suffer. You can scratch yourself or get cut. You can be bitten by a crawly, an insect of some kind, or a venomous snake. You can fall and hurt yourself, even break a bone. This is no lightweight matter. We're not going to the mall to go shopping. We're embracing the metaphys-ical experience of our existence. We will reach beyond the sense of things. What did you think this is? I thought that when I went on my vision quest, it was no serious thing. That I would just go to a park-like setting and everything would be fine.

"Maybe you should consider taking a solo vision quest on your own for an hour or so in the safety of your bedroom. This is a wilderness retreat vision quest. This is out in the wilderness, alone in the dark, listening to every sound.

"Trust me, spirits from the underworld are the lessons and they will come to speak to you. Lessons are the guidance that comes from your inner totems. They are the challenges that weaken your energy and cause you to fail, weaken, and dissolve. If you are scared of the dark, then it's a lesson. It comes to you from ignorance. Step into the dark and realize that it is only a deeper shade of blue or green, purple or burgundy. Realize that the ancient teachers are your spirit guides and they will show you through wisdom that all lessons are necessary.

"When I walked into my vision, I had to encounter the harshness of the dragon. I spent a day in the complexity of the dragon. There was no actual dragon in my desert. There was nothing there but me and sand and dirt and wind and heat, for I wasn't lucky enough to draw a vision quest on the side of a mountain. I had to do it in the heat of the desert. I learned that the heat of the desert was the breath of the dragon. I learned that that is Great Spirit. Not everything in life is easy. When you are reaching, you are learning. You cannot grow past your failures by standing in the same place.

"Your physical existence transforms at some point into the song of Grandmother Moon and the stories of Grandfather Sun, and the teachings of the sacred stars. You transcend through the call of your vision. You understand that you are in control. If you're lucky and your mental health is stable and your brain is intact chemically, then you can succeed in getting the answers you seek through a vision quest."

Dancing Spirit, the staff member in purple, speaks up.

"Let us remember, we are the ones who hurt ourselves. We're the ones who have chosen to scare ourselves. We're the ones who have chosen to be ill; we're the ones who have chosen not to listen when we're young and to perpetuate the lessons of the Lower World in our existence and walk in stupidity. We're the ones who entangled our lives with drugs and alcohol to defeat our health and destroy ourselves. Nothing comes from the Lower World but temptations, questions, disrespect, lessons, denial, defeat, and more along those lines. When we choose to glorify things that are empty and frail, then that's how our existence will be.

"I have seen through my vision snow and, through the power of the snow, I have gained great understanding of my life. Snow is soft and pretty; then when you get to the real side of it you can freeze to death, so not all that looks soft is safe. I remember I quested with a group of people who cared so much, they were going to stay together forever. They counted coup, which means they touched their fears and faced their visions with seven-colored sticks and put medicine words in their lives. Well, they're gone, and what remains in my heart is the glistening of the candles, the circle of colors I set off at night in the base camp medicine wheel, the place where I stood and realized that there's only one being—and that's me—who can hurt or heal me, who can release me, or contain me.

"You choose to be weak and so shall it be, and even weaker once you walk away from truth. Don't fear the monsters or the demons. Don't run from the anguish or the pain, but encounter the strength to stand in impassability and hold onto the ancient wisdom. As you come to the Spirit World and call for a vision, remember that the vision has called you, because you are sitting there waiting. The vision is the beginning of your letting go and walking into a safe way of living—knowing Creator has a path for you to follow and learning to live in the spirit ways of joy and strength."

Aho.

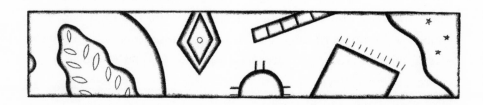

BEFORE YOU GET TO BASE CAMP

Your best vision quest teacher is yourself. There are also people you trust; they are staff members of a teacher in whose hands you have placed your life's dreams and hopes and ambitions. They are people who will guide you with the honesty and care that you need. It's important to be very careful about those you choose to vision quest with. Make sure the people are sound-minded and that the chemicals in their brains are balanced. They should have respect and compassion, and an understanding of spirituality. You want your teachers to understand the worlds—the Upper, Middle, and Lower Worlds—and to know that everything in the Lower World is called to show you your lessons. Bring yourself to a place where your journals and the words that you enter there are your teachers. Know that a vision guide instructor is simply someone who opens the door for you to encounter your personality and your mind, which are the voices of your spirit. Come to a place of balance by walking a spiritual road of goodness and beauty, to a place where you will find enlightenment and intelligence.

The best teachers that we have in vision quest are the wilderness totem bearers. Those are the wild animals, the crawlies, the winged ones, the swimmers, the tree people, the mineral people, water spirits, and earth spirits. We have walked a long time as human beings, listening to each other and telling others ourselves what to believe. We have built a country on the sacred indigenous land we know as Turtle Island, a place where we are to have freedom of spirituality, religion, and belief. Our teachers are the sky, the water, the fire, and the air we breathe.

If you choose to seek out a human teacher, this is a good thing, but remember that all humans make mistakes and they are learning just like you. Those who have led spiritual camps and taught in good ways, know the truths of human relationships and psychology, and they understand the human brain and mind.

When you seek out a vision quest leader or teacher, it's important that you connect with the teacher, that the person makes sense to you, and everything is open and honest between the two of you. There should be no evidence of drug or alcohol use from your teacher, nor should he or she have a criminal past.

At the Base Camp

If you are taking a retreat vision quest, a group vision quest, or going with a vision quest leader who has a staff, base camp is the place where you will set up camp and do your daily work and study.

This will be your home until the vision is over. The staff will be staying in the base camp when they are not "on point," meaning when a staff member is out with a visionary. You will start the quest in the base camp, where you will receive instructions and then leave for your individual vision site.

The base camp can be anywhere from two blocks to a mile and a half from your actual vision site. The base camp has a fire and a dry place for staff to relax and be comfortable. You'll be able to receive medical attention there, as well as train and interact with your fellow students when they come in from vision time. You'll spend three days in base camp getting ready for the vision—making tools, praying, asking questions. Then you will go out to your vision spot alone to set up your vision square and stay for whatever number of days have been decided on.

You must maintain the base camp in a respectful and sacred way, not taking too much wood for the fire, and complying with the rules of the state park or private land you're using.

BUILDING THE VISION QUEST ALTAR

The vision quest altar is set up in the base camp. All vision quest altars are built in the same way; it doesn't matter what kind of vision quest you are going to do.

1. Decide where you want to place the altar.
   a. It's good to place it by water, if you are outdoors and can find water to camp by.
   b. It needs to be in the center of the camp, as the camp is built around the altar.
   c. It should be out in the open where you can see the stars and the moon at night.

2. Consecrate the altar area.
   a. Clean the area by raking a circle 4 feet × 4 feet (1.22m).
   b. If you want to use a special stone for the altar, you can bring it from home or you can find one in the woods or by the water. The stone needs to be large and as flat a one as you can find. This is so you can set candles and objects on it. You can also use a flat piece of concrete purchased at a hardware store. At best, it should be 6 inches × 12 inches (15 × 30cm) long, and made of a material that will not burn.
   c. Place sage, cornmeal, and tobacco on the ground and pray for the spot to be sacred and clear, and full of light and good feelings from the Creator.
   d. Place the altar stone in the center of the circle. Pourclear, clean water over the stone—a full pitcher of water. The water is to bless and clean the stone and wake up the altar for use.
   e. Then find a stick that is 4 feet (1.2m) long and place it beside

the top of the altar on the left-hand side. Dig a hole and stand the stick in it. Place a white cloth on the pole. The cloth needs to be 24 inches (61cm) long and 7 inches (18cm) wide, made from 100 percent cotton. Place sage around the hole at the base of the stick to bless it. Pray for your vision as you build the pole.

3. **Place the ceremonial objects on the altar, which you will use as the vision quest goes on.**

   a. On the altar place four stones: one, a red-East-Spirit stone; the second a green-South-Emotions stone; third, a blue-West-Physical stone; and last, a white-North-Brain/Mind stone. These can be found where your vision quest takes place or you can bring them from home. The stones are to honor the four directions.

   b. A white candle in a safe fireproof holder to honor Great Spirit/Creator/God.

   c. A yellow candle in a safe fireproof holder to honor the creativity of the vision you will have.

   d. A purple candle in a safe fireproof holder to honor the wisdom of the vision you will have. These candles will be lit in prayer as the vision starts.

   e. All of you in the vision quest will place your medicine objects (jewelry, lucky charms, prayer objects, books, stuffed toys, cloths, pictures, and other special things) beside the candle on the ground as a small altar. The altar is a safe place where energy is contained; it will bring power to your tools.

   f. Place a good-sized stone on the ground. Use chalk to draw by hand a circle with a cross in the middle of it on the stone. This is your medicine wheel.

   g. Lay fresh flowers and herbs on the altar; they do not need to be in water. They are there as symbols of the circle of the quest, start to finish. Choose the kinds and colors of herbs and flowers (look up the meanings in the back of this book) and then journal them. They are a message from the vision.

4. Go to the altar before you leave for the vision quest and return to it when you are finished.

5. When the quest is done, take the altar apart.
Remove everything from the altar in the reverse order in which you placed it. Wash the stone and put it back in the woods or in a garden of your choice. If you want, you can keep the altar permanently in your home. (If you do the vision quest at home, you can leave the altar up and return to it to work with your vision in shamanic journey or prayer.)

BUILDING THE VISION SQUARE

The site of your sacred vision must be an area that is safe and that you have permission to use. You will need to listen to the instructions of your vision quest teacher or follow the instructions below to prepare it. The following list includes all the materials you will need to build a vision square.

1. Four stick poles 7 (2.1m) feet tall
2. Four pieces of 100 percent cotton cloth cut 3 inches (7.6cm) wide × 36 inches (1m) long, one in each color: red, green, blue, and white
3. White cord 27 feet (8.23m) long
4. Flowers and herbs of your choice
5. Rocks or pieces of wood to make your altar
6. A white candle to place on your altar
7. Tools such as drum and stones, and your prayer stick

Find an area that is about 10 feet (3m) wide × 20 feet (6m) long in which to place your vision square. You can set it up anywhere outdoors—in the wilderness, in the forest, in the desert. This is where you're going to perform your vision quest away from base camp. If you're doing a vision quest at home, you can also set up the square indoors.

When you have found the area in which to place your vision square, you need to offer tobacco and cornmeal to the ground. You will give away cornmeal, sage, and tobacco to this space. These are offerings to the Spirit World and to the ones who come to eat there.

Remember when you take your vision square apart to leave the area better than you found it.

1. Clean the area and place tobacco and cornmeal on the ground. Place sage on the ground to bless the area. (I like white sage or cooking sage for its wonderful smell. The spirits love that aroma.) Sprinkle water lightly on the ground to bless all.

2. Four poles, each 7 feet (2.1m) long, constitute the vision square. The poles, one for each direction, can come from a lumberyard or you can find them in the woods.

3. Make the vision square 4 feet (1.22m) × 6 feet (1.75m) long. Dig four holes in the ground and bury each pole one foot (31cm) deep—one in the East, one in the South, one in the West, and one in the North.

4. You also need four colored cloths: red for spirit; green for emotions; blue for physical; and white for the brain/mind.

5. You need a cord at least 27 feet (8.23m) long that will go all the way around the vision square. The cord needs to be white to represent the spirit.

6. Start in the East and tie the white cord to the pole 3 feet (1m) from the top. Go in a clockwise direction and tie the cord on the South pole, then the West, then the North. Finish by tying

it back at the East. Now, when you sit in the square, the cord is about head or shoulder high. The purpose of the cord is spiritually to contain the energy of the square.

7. Tie the red cloth on the white cord in the middle, between East and South, the green one between South and West, the blue one between West and North, and the white cloth between North and East.

Your vision square is now ready.

MAKING PRAYER TIES

To make your prayer ties, you will need

1. A blanket
2. Soft cloth or paper of 100 percent cotton (like napkins), in red or blue
3. Tobacco
4. Sage
5. Sweetgrass
6. Red yarn
7. A stick

Making a prayer tie is making a prayer.

First, lay out a blanket where you are going to work. This can be the place where you sit with your prayers.

Then, cut the cloth or colored paper. Use whatever color you wish, but I recommend 100 percent cotton cloth or paper in blue or red. Cut it into one-inch (2.5cm) squares. Prepare a square piece by laying it out flat.

Take a pinch of tobacco, sweetgrass, or sage, and place it in the center of the square.

Then, pull the corners up of the square, and gather and tie them with red yarn, making a pinch bundle.

Once your prayer ties are done, tie them onto a string or yarn, making a line.

Wrap the line around a stick...

and place it in a fire you have built outdoors. (If you are doing your ceremony at home, you can burn the prayer ties in a fireplace.) Let the smoke carry the prayers to Great Spirit.

Another alternative is to hang the line or drape it around a tree. This will allow deer to nourish themselves on the prayers. The deer is a carrier of prayer, as are the rain and sunshine.

VISION PRAYER

All peoples have their ways of prayer. This is good, for a vision is personal. I would like to share a prayer with you in case you don't have one or don't feel your prayers are heard.

"Heya, Grandmother/Grandfather Spirit/Creator/God. I feel you here looking at me, giving me the way and the understanding of spirit. I ask you to open my mind to your spirit voices that I might have a vision. I want to meet my guides and be shown the truth of a vision. I want my vision to come clear to me. I want to see your thoughts and path for my life.

"As I walk into the square, protect me from my own fears and from anything that might harm me. Bring the good of the vision to me and let me use it to bring a strong healing and a good walk to my life.

"Bless all the spirits and teachers who help me with this vision. Bless the Earth Mother as I sit with her and listen and see my vision. Thank you, Spirit, for the vision I will have. Guide me in the truth of the vision for the rest of my life. Aho."

· 4 ·

A Vision Quest Is the Voice of the Spirit World

"I have but one path left, the path of the vision. I have felt the blows of life and the pain burns like fire but I go on. I looked to drugs and women and there were no answers. I looked to money and the big spenders and high rollers and there were no answers there. I have crawled into crime and faced the dark God and all but sold my soul, and no answer to life was given to me. I climbed back to the road and looked for the sacred path. Great Spirit has called me to look to the Wolf. I hear the call."

—Lee

Lee is 40, a Native American mixed-blood male from Oklahoma. He has spent time in jail. He came from a poor life to a life of money and everything he needed.

He has shot and been shot. All his life he has been searching out counselors, looking for help. His problems started when he was eight and his mom died. He went to live with his Native American father and there he got into trouble with drugs and drink. He joined a gang in California, where he committed many crimes. He has had many scares and made many bad choices, but today he walks to Great Spirit with an open mind and willing heart.

It is night. Quiet settles around the meeting. I leave the teaching lodge and head for the fire pit. I see groups of students working with staff members. I walk up quietly beside the old pine tree and listen as Lee has a conversation with Jack Red Fox.

"How will I know if this vision quest is going to work? I have gone to many different kinds of rehab centers. I feel there are no answers for me," Lee says.

"Work is the question," Jack says. "Red is the answer to the question, for red holds within it seeking. Why do you seek, Lee? What do you think will help you in the vision quest?"

"Well, I've never been in a vision quest before. I was in jail with a man who was part Hispanic and part Native American. He was leaving the next week and told me that if I really wanted to get my life right, I would have to walk the Good Red Road. He explained to me that everything I was feeling was because of two things, my brain chemistry and my spiritual actions. I asked him what a vision quest is. I was very curious; was it a religious event? Had Jesus done it? What was it that he was talking about that might bring me peace of mind?

"The old man smiled at me and said, 'Vision quests are older than any type of religion. Yes, Jesus knew about a vision quest, for he went on one. He went out into the wilderness and faced his own fears. He was confronted by his devil. He was confronted by the grandest demon of all, Satan. In the Christian belief, Satan is the one who controls the mind.'"

I found this conversation very interesting, so I slipped on in and sat down beside Lee. He glanced at me and went on talking.

"From what I gathered, the direction I needed to take was a vision quest. So I spoke to other people and found out that Wolf Moondance was one of the better vision teachers in the area. I was referred to this camp so that I can face my fears, my monsters, and my demons."

Jack Red Fox nodded, "I remember that. I remember it very well. You see, I came to Wolf Moondance for the same reason. I needed to face my demons, my devils, my fears, and my anger. I was raised in a Catholic, Christian home. My father was a Christian minister and my mother was a Catholic. All my life, my father had gone to church and taught, but when he came home, he drank. An awful lot of drinking went on and a lot of pain was dealt out to the family members. It was very hard ever to trust in anything religious, because my father was such a hypocrite. I remember vividly the arguments and fights that my father and mother would have and then he would walk into the pulpit and preach the truth—according to the Gospel, as he put it. I had had enough and when I was 19, I hit the streets, and I hit the bottle and the pills, and I lived the ways of destruction and defeat. I was thrown in and out of different rehab programs and jails, until I was out of money and jobless. To make a long story short, I came to the lodge to find a better way than the therapists offered. I too was told that a vision quest would work for me. Everything about the vision quest was fine until I got into the darkness of the night, and then it happened. The worst monster of all confronted me. I spent the most fearful—the loneliest—night I have ever experienced in my existence. I felt things crawling on me. I knew that I was going to die. I was going to get eaten by an animal. Something or someone was going to come and slit my throat. It didn't matter. I had every negative thought there was, and more than once I was going to bust the string and run out of my vision square down the hill through the base camp, down the road and back to town for one more drink.

"I stood up, getting ready to leave the vision square, and it confronted me. I can call it 'it' because that fits it best of all. 'It' was large; it was shadowy; it was black; it was red-eyed; and it pushed me with both hands on my chest. I fell back into my vision square and it stood there snarling. Its eyes were piercing, deep-set; it had wrinkles in its forehead, a long chin, pointed ears, scraggly hair, and pointed teeth like a vampire's. It stared at me and raised its long, thin hand with long fingernails that bent at the ends. The thing challenged me to come past it. I spent at least 45 minutes trying to get nerve enough to run past it. Then I realized I could turn around and run the other way. Bam! I ran right into another one. I turned back, and bam, there was another. I turned again, bam! Bam! In every inch of the circle were these hideous monsters and smaller ones, demons that lurked behind the tall ones. They all snarled and growled. The noise became overwhelming. My head was spinning. Behind them stood my father with his Bible in his hand.

"'Simply turn to Christ, simply turn to Christ and it will all be okay,' I could hear him say. I put my hands over my ears and drew my knees up under my chin and put my face down between my knees. I couldn't take anymore.

"'Please stop!' I shouted. I didn't look because I didn't want to see any more yellow slime or blood oozing from anything. And then it stopped.

"I just sat there quiet and listened to the wind. I heard a voice say, 'Are you ready? Are you ready to let go?'

"I was ready. I wanted it all to go away. I wanted the morning to come and I wanted the staff person who was assigned to me to come and take me out of the square. I sat very still because I knew if I looked up, I would be confronted by my own monsters and devils once more. I sat there until my legs went to sleep.

"Finally, I just rolled over on my side and covered myself with my medicine blanket and began to sob. You see, Lee, you must confront yourself in that small space, in that small period of time. For a vision quest to work, you must walk past what you fear the most," Jack said.

Lee shook his head. "I don't know that it will be that easy for me. I really think I'll bolt home past the devil and head straight back into its mouth, because as I sit here right now, I don't know if I can make it or not. I don't know what will happen when I go in my vision square. I'll probably sit there for hours on end and nothing will happen. You know, friends of mine had great things to say about their vision quest, that they had seen their future and dealt with their past, and understood that they had risen at sunrise and felt reborn. My biggest fear is death itself, the death of my soul. What if it's already gone?" Lee asked.

"If it were gone, Lee, you wouldn't be sitting here between Wolf and me. You would not be gazing into the fire longing for tomorrow. You would have given up and run deeper into the darkness. A lot of people come to the vision square and they don't have darkness. They have only kindness and light. I've seen that also. But for us who are chased by our demons and afflicted by drug use and addiction to alcohol, breaking laws and being mean to other people, it's not that easy, because we have to walk the long road of recovery.

"After that night, I realized what detoxify really was. I detoxed in my square. I found my inner spirit. I stood in what my inner totem was and began to walk full of power and success, offering hope to other people. I stayed on with Wolf because she needed help, and I'm still here volunteering my time. I have a home and a family, I have a job, and I have it all because of the night that I confronted my demons and monsters in that square."

"That is definitely what I want to achieve," Lee says. "I don't know that it would be that easy for me, because the demons don't have faces. I can't really say what I'm looking at when I feel empty and alone, what the thing is that makes me use."

Jack Red Fox looked at him and said, "It's your choice. One of the things you learn from your vision is the voice of the sacred stars. Because you're connected to the vision of Wolf Moondance, you walk with the same teachings. We have choice in our medicine wheel. When you get to the base camp, you'll connect with Rainbow Medicine, and there you can pick up the principles it takes to start filling in some of the emptiness."

Lee looked at Jack and nodded his head as if he understood.

"There is a lot of work to do and a lot of time left to do it," I said. "Don't push yourself so hard. Understand that the vision square is a time of joy, a time of peace, a time to settle confusion. As we study, as we walk along the path together looking for the vision, we'll come to that place." I put my arm around Lee.

"Thanks for your help, Wolf Moondance, and thank you, Jack Red Fox," Lee said.

Jack Red Fox nodded, got up, and walked off.

"I think things will be just fine. A vision quest has a tendency to do that for you," I say.

Aho.

INTENTIONS FOR A VISION QUEST

It is said that people go out and sit with the wilderness and come back and say they went on a vision quest. I want to pass along an interpretation of vision quest that I like to teach as well as live with.

If you walk blindly in this life, then you will have a blind outcome. If you just let things happen, they just happen. When we question why our lives don't go like someone else's, or the way we want it to go, we must question our intentions.

Sometimes we follow someone else: we listen to an elder and we become what that elder says. Or we act like a hero whom we admire, or a favorite person. We mimic other people; we learn from other people because we think that what they know is right. We're guided and directed by parents and grandparents, aunts and uncles, brothers and sisters.

But really, whose life is it? Isn't it funny how human beings herd together like cattle? If it's a good concert, everybody wants to go. If it's a good baseball game, everybody wants to be involved. If it's a good movie, everybody wants to see it. If it's a nice car, everybody wants to own one.

Where is our individuality? That's where the intentions of a vision quest come in. We learn from our vision, therefore we are learning from the spirit voice of Great Spirit, Creator. When you set your intentions for a vision quest, I would like you to answer the following questions. Take out your journal and a pen. Find a quiet place where you won't be bothered and sit and write.

Questioning Your Intentions for a Vision Quest
1. Do you believe you had a life before this one? If so, what was it like?
2. In having that life and knowing what that life was like, how does it guide you in your human existence?

3. What is beauty to you? List some beautiful things. What do they mean to you? How might they guide you?
4. What is your purpose in having a vision quest? What do you want to achieve? What do you want to learn about yourself?
5. List your needs in life.
6. What are your wants? What's the difference between a need and a want?
7. How long will you be connected to your vision?
8. What are some of your favorite things to do? How do they guide you?
9. What is the most important thing you know about yourself? How did you learn it?
10. Why do you exist as a human being?
11. What would you enjoy doing every day for the rest of your life? What kinds of things do you need to do to make you a happy person?
12. What is happy?
13. What is your favorite element—snow, wind, sunshine, rain, or something else?
14. Who's in charge of your spirit? Who's in charge of your life?
15. Why would you give away your life to someone else? Would you?
16. What is love to you?
17. How much do you know about the Spirit World? How do you intend to learn about it?
18. What do you think will keep you from achieving your vision? Why?
19. What is your greatest talent?
20. What does your spirit look like? What would you call it? What spirit name would you give yourself?
21. Do you have a spirit guide?
22. What do you know about spirit guides?

23. How will you interpret your vision?
24. Where will you go to find the answers and how long do you think it will take to understand the answers of the vision quest as a personal spiritual path?

A vision quest leader—or you, if you are going on a solo vision quest—must gather information from the 24 questions above about your intentions. It is important that you answer them as honestly and clearly as you can.

Next, see the following steps for building your vision square.

· 5 ·

Vision Quest Ceremony

"I have called on God for help many times in my life and felt I got answers. I have always believed in prayer, have lived a good life full of obedience, but there has always been something missing. I have never known which way to go to find what's missing; then I listened to the rocks and the wind and heard the call of the spirit."

—Cathy

Cathy, age 35, comes from Kansas. She was raised on a farm, worked hard to get an education, and is now a high school teacher, which had been her dream. She has always had a need to know about spirit. She went to church for many years until an incident occurred that she could not reconcile with her belief. She and some other young women arrived early for choir practice to find the preacher, who was married, kissing the piano player, who was also married. She lost faith in the preacher and left the church.

She followed the spiritual side of life and started studying the ways of crystals and spirit guides. She met a very special person, who was a student of Rainbow Medicine, who led her to Wolf Moondance. She is now fulfilling her desire to have a spiritual experience.

The time is evening, the time I like to gather the students together and go over the journey of vision quest, the journey of sacred knowledge. The staff has gathered the students together and they are ready to study. Evening holds the beauty of the sunset. This is a closing time, time to finish one thing and bring another to start. It is the time of the stars, the ones who see and speak to us of the ways of the Spirit World.

A small fire has been built; the trucks are packed, and the gear is ready to go. There's not a lot to pack. We don't have to take much to set up base camp, but what we need is prepared. So after the students spend a couple of days gathering their vision square materials, we'll be off to base camp to do our ceremony of vision.

There's great anticipation in their faces as I walk up and sit on the log. My seven assistants in their red, orange, yellow, green, blue, purple, and burgundy shirts step into the staff commitment by standing behind the students. They simultaneously tie a burgundy cord on their left arm. This represents the fact that they are committed and tied in with the students on the vision quest. They will wear the cord until they bring the students back, all feeling safe as they walk out into the world with their new vision. Then they will join me when I present the spirit name that each visioning student brings forth as his or her new, clean inner-self name.

It is a beautiful evening. The sun has drifted to sleep and the evening colors of blue have joined us once again.

"Grandmother, Grandfather, I am so grateful for the stars that I see. Thank you for giving us a silver glitter path to follow. Thank you for building us a bridge on which we can cross into the arms of your gentle breeze. Kiss our cheeks with your knowledge. I present to you John, Lee, Cathy, Linda, and the seven staff members of the Sacred Seven Star Lodge, myself Wolf Moondance, and our wolf, Chimi, who will accompany us. We come to you now asking for the ceremony of vision."

I open my eyes and look at the students. They are sitting, holding tight the medicine blankets that are wrapped around them.

"Loosen up, kids. Don't be so tight," I say. "This is the experience of a lifetime, a time where you step forward and talk to Great Spirit, a time when nothing can get to you."

"But that's not true," Linda says. "What about the Underworld, the place where our deepest temptations and fears come from. How am I ever going to break free from my fears? There are monsters that have been hiding under my bed for years and they're coming to eat me."

"Eat you?" John says. "How can a fear eat you?" He looks at her with intensity.

"Well, that's easy," Making Words, the blue staff member says. "A fear totally destroys your mind by keeping you from having what you want, by tempting you, and breaking down your daily processes. I learned that in Rainbow Medicine when I took the Quest for the Whole Self. I learned it from Wolf as a destruction of balance. Each one of us has the chance to set forth our intentions, to learn the lessons of opportunity and discipline, and to go forth and have a good life, but our fears are the monsters under our beds. Tonight, Linda is very scared and we need to do something to help her."

Cat Eyes, the green staff member, shakes her head. "I was chased for years by a dark spirit that escaped from a Ouija board. I believed that nonsense. I believed that I could be sitting with a wonderful oracle tool and conjure up an evil spirit and have it chase me for the rest of my time. Then I finally came to the understanding that all I had to do was sit down and do a ceremony to release it: take some fresh creek water and throw it over my head and let the thought go as the drops of water hit the ground."

Pepper Dog says, "Let me tell you that the vision you will achieve—or a vision anyone has already achieved, or any type of spiritual instruction that guides us—gives us the ability to have a great life.

"I didn't take my vision lightly. I had experienced childhood abuse, with broken bones and a broken heart. I was a teenager; it was easy to hit the road and take drugs. It was easy to lose myself on a motorcycle and cross the country thinking that was what life was, a free-spirited ride from one coast to the other. It wasn't until I encountered Rainbow Medicine and understood the value of vision questing that I began to realize that everybody has a vision."

Pepper Dog stands up. "We've packed our trucks, we've got our gear, and we've got our allowance of food and water. We've got our drums, and the things it takes to make fire, and our medicine blankets," she said. "We've got the tools it takes to keep us safe in those moments when we walk away from the real world, as we call it. I have found that the real world is actually the Spirit World. I have found that the things that are spiritual and bring forth my life in a good way, and that teach me how to have honor and patience and respect, are the real world. I think of the world that we live in as the fake world—a world of confusion, a world of war, of argument, of racism, of eating and drinking poison. Let's step forth into the ceremony of the vision and walk into the real world—the Spirit World, where the stars speak and the moon is our direction and Grandmother looks at us and says, 'Watch the sun and open the doors to the spirit, the emotions, the physicality, and the mental planes.' It is a place where trees and rivers talk, rocks speak, and colors sing the truth of all. When you take a vision quest, you are questing for the vision, which is the voice of your spirit.

"Don't be afraid of your monsters and the things you conjure up in your head, and don't think about old rituals that belong to other people."

"Yes," I nod. "These are choices that we make, and when you come back here from that vision square, you are going to be as different as you make yourself to be. I have hard work every day. It doesn't matter what I'm doing, healing or teaching, or writing or raising children, or teaching grandchildren—it doesn't matter—I have to reach deep inside the vision and structure outlines. I have to listen to the lessons of organization and discipline. I have to look life in the face and have faith.

"I say to you that the ceremony of vision is a simple one. You build a sacred vision square, make prayer ties, and hang them on your prayer lines. You stay there until your vision appears or until time runs out, attended to by the staff members. Rest and listen, look and find, journal, come out of the square, take it all down, bring it all to the fire and let it go. That is the ceremony of vision the way I teach it—from the sun, moon, and the seven stars—which was given to me by Great Spirit, and which I've walked with to this very day, heading into being an elder.

"I look back on a whole lifetime of students and programs, of creeks and rivers and ponds where people have come to wash away their pain, to be submerged, and rise in the clean, clear breath of air that is given to us each day as a fresh new opportunity by Great Spirit. I want you each now to go forth and gather the tools it takes to build your sacred vision circle. Butterfly Sky, would you pass out the list to the students?"

The staff member in yellow gives the students sheets that tell them what they need to build a sacred vision square (see the list on page 77). As Butterfly Sky distributes the instructions, the four students take them and read them over. They understand the pieces of cloth they need, the cord they need, and how to choose the herbs and flowers. They understand and sit quietly, looking at each other. They realize they haven't grown up together. They haven't lived together their whole lives or raised their children together. They barely know each other. They are four people coming from different avenues of life, looking for their personal vision. They may never see or speak to one another again. But they feel the spirit bond they share. Each one has pain and fear—that is the bond between them. They each know that the vision is a mystery to which they will open the door and that they will walk their lives with the bond of a vision. They feel the excitement of losing the fear of pain and finding the truth of spirit in the visions they will have.

They exchange smiles, stand, and give each other hugs. I dismiss them for the evening. They have two days to gather the objects they need. The staff of Rainbow Medicine and I are ready to embark upon the vision quest, the magical healing that lies ahead.

Aho.

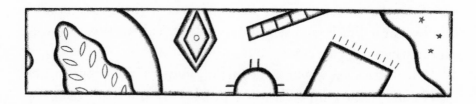

SEEKING A VISION

By the time you are ready to understand the calling of a vision, you have done a lot of preparation work. I would like to help you to understand the calling of a vision by breaking it down into five parts.

1. What a calling is.

When you need something and spirit hears, it sends you a knowing, and this is the beginning of a calling.

The main calling in human life is a vision, for it is the path map of your life. Your vision is the knowledge of your purpose. Without your personal vision you are separated from your spirit understanding. Physical life is very hard for humans and it takes a lot of work to understand your purpose in it. As humans, we are all open to control; we can be led away from the truth to follow the ways and teachings of others. There are no teachings you should follow but the pure truth. As you grow in years of life, you come to think you are following the truth, when what has happened is that you have started following the teachings of others' fear and need to control. The call or calling of your vision comes to open up your mind to the feelings that guide you through the physical test known as life.

A calling is the voice of Great Spirit and all that guides you from the Spirit World. In your feelings you are hearing from spirit; through touch, smell, taste, sight, and sound; you hear spirit, see spirit, and know spirit. All is spirit and your feelings tell you so. In the spiritual realm, you have the same sight, sound, taste, hearing, smell, and touch that you do in the physical, along with emotions, which are reactions. Emotions are the physical reactions of a human being, and feelings are the spirit actions.

When the calling comes for a personal vision, the human is ready to get his or her spiritual senses intact. It can take place any time from the ages of four to 18. All humans have the call to understand their spiritual senses. It is up to the parent to teach and share the truth about that vision. If you do not understand your personal vision, you have a feeling of loss in your life, and a lot of confusion and emptiness.

Great Spirit gives an understanding of all that is faith, and your faith is the ability to see: that sight is your vision. The vision is an understanding through a spiritual code.

All humans love to see the personal beauty of animals and to have them in their lives. The love of wildlife is related to a longing for the freedom the animal has. This physical experience connects humans to their animal totems and gives them a relationship to the spiritual animal being.

2. Why you have a calling from your personal vision.

It is a wake-up call. Your vision is the piece in life that you're missing. A personal vision is the calling to remember spirit. From the time you're four years of age, you need to know and remember the Spirit World. If you are not acquainted with the spiritual, you will be scared. It would seem that there is a reason for this knowledge to be missing in your life—and there is. When greed and fear are at hand, control becomes an issue, and that happens when you do not remember and do not have ways to learn.

If you look at history, you will see that control has always been the main source of energy. In the attempt to obtain control and importance, humans often forget their vision of life. One of the reasons there is spiritual death and physical sickness is because most humans do not have a vision.

Humankind once knew the truth and then the emotions came into play—mainly the emotion of fear. All the meanness in life arises out of fear. Jealousy is fear. This is all a part of the lessons of life that we must work hard to understand. It is really easy to understand life if you are taught and if you listen. We as humans are taught that there is truth and we should be honest and good. Then we see that humans do not do as they teach. In using the phrase "we're only human," we pardon all that we do that is not true, good, and right. Our spirit is not able to live with that.

It is a simple thing to see that, in our lives, we are as we believe. That also means we are what we think, and since we are chemical and electrical, we are what we do. We are also what we eat, and our energy is affected by this truth. If you think you are someone special because of what you have, then you will do anything to have what you want. You are entrusted early in life to a parent to guide you and teach you how to remember. If the parent does not teach you your spiritual needs, you will suffer until you understand your spirit and your part here on earth.

We are half spirits living as humans. The purpose of human life is to remember that we are not separated from Great Spirit. We are here in this material form to remember our spirit selves. In your personal vision you will find your story andyour needs. We each have to understand and make sense of our whole spirit life to understand the vision we walk with on the Earth Mother.

3. Spiritual reasons for a vision quest in your physical life.

a. We as humankind need to remember we were spirit before we were human. We need to remember the calm quiet peace.

b. We as humankind need contact with Great Spirit. We need to see a vision and have the answers come to us from Great Spirit. It gives us an opportunity to understand the guidance of the Spirit World.

c. Often, we have been separated from our spiritual truths and we search for answers from others. There can be much abuse from others in our lives as they try to guide us. As we listen through prayer and see and hear that the Creator cares and has a path map—a vision—for us, then we know there is love from the spirits for us and we have faith and hope.

d. Each one of us needs a vision, goals, and dreams. We need the honor of the truth of Creator and the stories of others who have followed their vision.

4. Steps to becoming physically ready for your vision.

In order to have a vision, you must be ready in the brain and the mind. You will need a journal, a pen, and quiet time to answer the questions asked of you. If you have a problem writing, use a tape recorder and answer that way, or you can read the questions aloud and answer them aloud, so that you hear your thoughts.

A big part of being on the right path to your vision is knowing the answers that the vision will provide you over time. When you live with a vision, you need to know what you think and believe. Your vision is the voice of your spiritual path and all guidance comes from your understanding of that inner knowing.

    a. Are you ready for the vision to call? Do you have the time set aside in your life to work with your vision? If so, when? How long each day will you study and work with your vision?

    b. Are you sound and healthy? Many times in life we hear things or see things that are caused by a chemical problem. Do you know if you are mentally healthy? Have you spoken to a counselor or seen a psychiatrist and do you know you are healthy?

    c. Have you spoken in prayer to your higher power and know this is the right path for you?

    d. Do you know that a vision is for all people no matter what their bloodline or belief?

    e. Are you resting and sleeping well? Getting enough rest is essential. It is very important that you are not desperate or coming to your vision out of human need, but that the vision itself is calling you to understand and see it clearly.

    f. What is the reason you want a vision?

    g. Where does your spiritual knowledge come from? Do you need to study and have a sound knowledge base?

    h. How do you become spiritual?

    i. Are you spiritual or religious?

j. When you have your vision, how will you be different?

k. What do you read? Fact or fiction?

l. Do you want to belong to a group who believe as you do?

m. How do you feel about this teaching? Do you know it is right for you? How?

Answer those statements and questions in your journal, or in any way you wish. When you have read and listened to yourself, go through the questions once more and make sure you understand and can fill in all the answers in your own way and feel good about them. See if any of your answers has changed. As you work with the idea of the calling of a vision, you are getting ready to move on to the ceremony of finding the vision.

5. How you know a vision is calling.

There are several ways to know the call of a vision.

First, let me explain vision. It is the path map of your life. It will be a picture of your feelings. It will include color, symbols, and characters, such as spirits, animals, elements, plants, and landscapes. It is a source that comes directly from Great Spirit, which helps you understand your purpose in life.

Here are several ways you know you are being called by your vision:

a. You see pictures in your thoughts that seem like daydreams. They will look like hand-painted pictures in your thoughts.

b. You will come into contact with objects you think about or have thought about all your life. Example: a rushing river, a rainbow over a hill, an eagle, or a bear paw print.

c. You feel empty and lonely and as if there is more to life, but you cannot find the "more."

d. You feel drawn to some place or objects and do not know why.

e. You know there is something you need to know, but can't remember what it is.
f. You feel you belong somewhere else but do not know how to find where that is.
g. You see a place in your mind—a place you have never been— and you can't remember where it is.
h. You feel there are others like you, but you don't know where they are or how to find them.
i. You have your beliefs and they aren't like everyone else's. You know they are real and good and that there are others somewhere who have the same thoughts.
j. You have a dream, but you don't dream it at night—you just know it.
k. You are drawn to special animals, and know and feel they have something you need to know.
l. There are special colors that you have always liked and feel are your colors.
m. Finding a purpose is hard for you.

These are ways you know you are being called to have a vision. It is important to know, if you don't already, that a vision is very important to your life, that it is a personal thing, and that you must trust in yourself to find it. It is dangerous to give your power to others and let them interpret your vision unless they are visionaries or your spiritual teachers. You can reach out in many ways, but you and only you can make sense of your vision.

In understanding the ceremony of vision, you will prepare the way for it.

· 6 ·

The Breath of the Vision

It is 6:00 a.m. The four students, Lee, John, Cathy, and Linda, meet at the lodge, along with the seven staff members, my half-side Raven, my wolf Chimi, and me. We check to make sure the staff has everything they need and that the students have gathered their poles, flags, and cords, packed in a special bag, and everything else they need—herbs, flowers, and stones—to make their sacred squares. They are ready to embark on their vision quest.

We blindfold the students and load up the van to travel to our sacred base camp that is hidden away.

"What is the purpose of the blindfold?" Lee asks.

There is no answer in the van.

"May I ask what is the purpose of the blindfold? I am curious," Linda says.

"Remember," a voice says.

We travel quite a ways and there is no further answer.

Then Making Words, the staff member in blue, begins to speak. "You are blindfolded because you don't need to see in the physical world. You are being taken to a sacred place, the Seven Star base camp, for vision questing. You will never go there again and you do not need to know where you are on this earth. It is important that, when you go on your vision quest, you be in a place where you let go of all knowledge of physicality. When I went on my vision, I was taken to a sacred base camp too. Wolf Moondance uses a different camp quite often. Where you go proves that you are strong in your trust."

"I don't understand why I can't see where I'm going," John says. "What if something goes wrong and I need help?"

"That's what we are here for," says White Mouse, the staff member in orange. "We're here to see to it that you are fine."

"We're also here to see to it that you use your creativity and reach beyond your fears and draw from your vision," Butterfly Sky, the staff member in yellow, says. "It's time that you let go of your childhood fears, your childhood panics, your childhood abuse."

"Walk past your adult abuses and have confidence," says Jack Red Fox.

"There is nothing and no one who can hurt you," Pepper Dog says.

"I need everyone to be still," I say. "We must be quiet and listen to the breath of the vision."

"How do we do that?" John asks.

There is no answer—only stillness. We hear only the tires and the cars going past us.

"Rise above the noises of the physical world and listen to the breath of the vision."

We come to the sacred land of the base camp, pull in, park, and unload the students. We stand them in a square, back-to-back.

"Listen for the breath of the vision," I tell the students.

"I don't understand what you want from us," John says.

I do not answer. I simply begin to pray quietly.

"Creator, Grandmother, Grandfather Spirit, help each one who stands here at this moment to listen for your breath, to begin to let go of physicality. Let each one of them hear the silence."

"I hear the wind," Linda says. "I can hear voices in the wind. Listen, John, and you'll hear them," she says.

The four students stand quietly as the vision staff go about setting up camp, building a fire in the fire pit, preparing the vision lodge for teachings, and getting ready for the four students to go about their vision quest.

The staff members set up a large, round tent where we can all get in out of the elements, if necessary. They put down cedar inside the tent and place the sacred vision pole outside the door.

"Quietly breathe in and out," Cat Eyes, the green staff member, says to the four vision students. "Breathe in through your nose and out through your mouth for the breath of the vision."

Soon, I see the four vision students and Cat Eyes breathing together. All four students take a breath in and out at the same time.

"I think you have it, I know you have it," I say to them. "Can you feel the breath of the vision?"

"Yes," Lee says.

"I can," Linda says.

"Yes," John says.

"I do," Cathy says.

They breathe very quietly and softly. We remove the blindfolds and the students look straight ahead. They are at peace within their own minds. Cat Eyes hands the students their vision square bags.

"Each staff member will take you now on a hike where you will look for your place. Remember the shamanic journey that you have had and you will know your place. They will take you out as noon comes upon us. When you find your place, you will build your vision square.

"Then you will go inside it and work with your vision until your staff member calls time and tells you to return. At that time, you will take down your vision square and bring it all back and place it in the center fire, which is over there." I motion to the fire pit where Pepper Dog, the staff member in burgundy, and my half-side Raven have built the fire. It now has a beautiful flame rising six feet in the air.

"After you have burned everything that has to do with your vision, you will go to the vision teaching lodge and sit in the tent and journal. We will have meetings back at the teaching lodge, to see if there are questions. Does everyone understand?"

"We do, I do, we all do, yes," they say.

"Good." I remove my black hat, place it on my heart, and run my hand down my medicine sash, a garment I have earned. It is made of leather, and the levels of study and teaching I have completed are hand-beaded on the leather. I grip my walking cane tightly.

"Grandmother/Grandfather, aho. I ask that these students walk into the Spirit World and to their vision, and that they do not return without reaching their goal, their personal vision. I ask that everything and everyone be with them, that they walk carefully into shamanic journey and stay in the Upper World where the teachers will speak to their ears. I call for their visions. We will remain here in camp and drum quietly and be in prayer. Watch over the students. Aho."

I put my black hat back on and look at the students. "Remember your vision square. String your prayer ties on the cords of your vision square. Step into the vision square from the East. Your staff member will then offer a prayer and leave you alone. You will be alone until the staff member returns. You may leave."

Jack Red Fox takes John; White Mouse, the orange staff member takes Lee; Making Words, the blue staff member takes Cathy; and Dancing Spirit, the purple staff member takes Linda. They walk the students away in four different directions, and disappear into the wilderness.

"It is incredible," I think, as I watch the students walk away. "Incredible, they have reached the honor of being whole and complete. They are in the perfect spiritual balance."

In the years that have passed, I have helped many walk on the path to find their vision.

"Grandmother/Grandfather, I give thanks for this opportunity, for all the students who have come to find their vision. Aho."

VISION SQUARE BREATHS

BREATH #1—INVITING THE VISION

Sit quietly in your vision square, facing the East. Breathe in through your nose and out through your mouth. Pray to Great Spirit to allow you to have a vision.

Turn to the South and breathe in through your nose and out through your mouth. Ask Great Spirit to balance your emotions, so that you might let go of your human thoughts and listen with your spirit mind.

Turn to the West and breathe in through your nose and out through your mouth. Ask Great Spirit to keep your physical body safe and allow you to endure, so that you might have a vision.

Turn to the North. Breathe in through your nose and out through your mouth. Listen. Ask Great Spirit to forgive any human faults you might have and to bless the worthiness within your spirit. Then take a deep breath in through your nose and out through your mouth four times and relax.

BREATH #2—THE BREATH OF YOUR VISION GUIDES

Stand in your vision square and hold your arms straight up above you. Breathe in through your mouth and hold your breath. As you hold it, ask to see your spirit guides. Hold your breath as long as you can until you see in your mind's eye a spirit guide. Let your breath go when you can hold it no longer and breathe in deeply through your mouth again, looking for your spirit guides.

You see more of them—there might be a winged one or a two-legged one. There may be a light being. In any case, you will see your guides. Let your breath go, sit down gently and journal what you have seen.

BREATH #3—THE BREATH OF YOUR PROTECTORS

Lie on the ground in your vision square, face down. Breathe in and out easily, praying to the earth that you will be safe, that you are no longer bound to physicality and that you let go of all that is physical. In your mind's and spirit's eye, you see your protecting beings. They will be lights, they will be of different colors. When you have seen them, rise and journal your protectors' images.

BREATH #4—THE BREATH OF OLD WOMAN ROCK

Sit cross-legged, facing East. Breathe in through your mouth seven times and out through your nose each time. Before you, you see a dirt path. Follow that path until you see a tiny old woman covered by a blanket. She is Old Woman Rock. When you reach the spirit, she will guide you into the Spirit World and take you to see your vision. You are on your own to do as you need. Take nothing back from the Spirit World. Keep nothing except your vision.

When Old Woman Rock has guided you to your vision, she will say goodbye by nodding, and you will thank her and let her go. Then come back to your vision square and journal your vision.

✳   ✳   ✳   ✳   ✳

The breaths of the vision are my personal teachings, given to me by my mother, Marie Screaming Eagle. I give them to you to use in solo or group vision questing. I do not attribute them to any traditional belief other than my own family's. I do not call them part of a Native American ceremony—or anyone's ceremony. I want the freedom of the ceremony to speak for itself. It is strictly from Great Spirit, passed on from my mother to me to you, and from you to whoever needs it.

Note to the Reader

This ceremony is never to be sold. It is only to be given away. As you have purchased this book, you have purchased pages of hard work, but the ceremony of the breaths is a gift.

For every humankind there may come a call that impels us to leave behind our work and the people in our lives and go off alone for a short time to look within and discover our spiritual sides and our selves in the circle of life. You can hear it calling. You feel a general unease: something is missing; some unspecified trouble in your life nags at you; you want a change.

The answer is the vision quest.

These questions unconsciously arise: "Who am I?" "What do I have to give?" "How can I heal my wounds?" "Where do I go when I die?" "What is the reason for life?" You know these are questions you must answer, despite your fears.

When this calling comes, it is time to make a vision quest. You make the choice and find the teacher or leader, or you go on a solo vision quest. You learn about the terrain in the area you choose or you decide to quiet your home and vision there.

You study the ancient symbols and teachings that will help you along your way. Get to know the meanings of the animals, colors, flowers, herbs, and minerals (they can be found in the back of this book).

The vision quest has been called a rite of passage and has been important to the health of human societies for thousands of years, enabling humankind to negotiate its self-understanding with purpose and meaning. As you vision, you discover the gifts of the inner self that bring a deep peace to the whole self and to your daily life. You open your mind to the higher spirit of the Creator.

As you go on the vision quest, you see life as a movie for which you are the scriptwriter. You have the teaching of the vision and the guides as they come; there is the completion of an old life and the new realization of the path of truth you seek. As you find the vision and return to the world reborn, you can set goals and get answers to your questions. A vision quest can tell you:

1. Who you are.
2. What you are.
3. What you want from life.
4. Where you came from.
5. Who your spirit guides are.
6. Clues to your spirit name—and even the name itself (if you ask for it and listen to the guides, or if the teacher hears it in prayer and gifts you with it).
7. A rebirth from the old habits and ways and a change of lifestyle, as you lay out new goals and new ways of thinking.

· 7 ·

The Students Relate Their Visions

The students go to their squares and start their vision quest. The squares are built as spaces where the students can be alone. It is important for the students to be undisturbed so they can make contact with the Spirit World. They enter the vision square at sunset and stay until the teacher sends for them. The amount of time will be determined by the teacher. It can be a few hours or up to four days. The students are brought out of the square on the fourth day, at sunset.

As they experience their time in the vision square, they all have stories to tell.

John's Vision

"I stepped into the vision square with my drum and prayer stick and medicine blanket. I sat in the square and my first thoughts were that this was really dumb. What do I need to sit here for? This went on for a long time. I had no watch so I didn't know how long.

"I thought about school and all the times in my life I had to sit and listen or do things I didn't care about. I sat a while more and fell asleep. It was as I slept that I met a wonderful spirit, Odo. He was both human and spirit 'cause he was green-skinned. He took me to my childhood and showed me the pain I suffered. He showed me that people are human and can make mistakes and be very mean also. He showed me the drinking and the anger my parents had and how they fought and hurt me and my brothers.

"It was very hard for me in those days. I remember the pain my father caused, the beatings and belittlement I suffered. Then he showed me the childhood of my drunken father and the pain he had undergone. It could be thought of as a dream, but Odo told me it was not a dream—I was just in a rest state where the pain would not hurt me. He told me he would always be there and could help me.

"I woke the next morning feeling open and wanting to see Odo. I was not hungry, I felt at peace and full. I drummed and prayed for my vision. Most of the days were spent with memories of pain and anger. I felt I was never going to have a vision, one that could change my life. I would pray and drum and cover myself with my blanket and rest. The staff dropped off water and I loved the feeling of people caring.

"As I slept during one session, Odo called me to a gentle creek that was running fast and clear. He was standing beside the creek and there were bright blue flowers beside him. 'These are your medicine, their color speaks of Truth; you must understand the truth,' Odo said. 'Look at life and know it was hard. You now need to live in the moment, not in the past. You need to come to a clear understanding of your vision. It is the medicine that helps you know Creator cares and wants healing and peace for you.'

"I had to see the beauty of the blue flowers—they were irises—and I need to understand what Odo has told me and live in the moment.

"I heard the sound of fire crackling and the smell of food cooking. Odo told me that was the center of my personality and that I was a good person, strong, loving, and caring. I need to walk away from the fear and be my whole self.

"The days and nights all ran together. I quit trying to make sense of it and just went with the feelings. Each minute felt like years and everything I could think of came to mind.

"But then the most wonderful thing happened. I met Odo and I saw my vision. It was a creek with trees along it. There was a large rock in the middle of the creek. I looked close at the rock and it showed me a picture, like a TV. Things I needed to work on and things that could happen if I did not change.

"Odo said I was blessed. I was shown a spirit guide and animal guides. When they came for me, I felt new and released, reborn to the mystery of my vision."

Cathy's Vision

"I went to the vision square and placed my spirit stick and stones in a wheel. I covered myself with my blanket. I tried to sleep to pass the time but I heard an owl. I thought the owl was real, but then in a while I realized the owl was different and I was in a different place. I looked around me and there were lots of people and things that were ugly and smelled. They would take runs at the cords of my square. I was so scared and wanted to leave, but I cried and hollered out for help. Soon I realized that I was in another world and no one was coming. This went on for a long time. I saw buildings burning and people dying and these mean things eating people. Oh, I wanted this to stop and I wanted to run away! I spent what felt like days watching blood dripping from a tree. I hoped this was not my vision.

"I wanted to run. I sat and prayed and did not open my eyes for hours, when all at once I saw a dust storm of colored sand—red, orange, and blue. I saw my husband and children walking in the dust. Also many animals, a black horse, a cat, a dog, and a fish. Then a large ugly thing ate them, and I screamed and cried for hours.

"Then I began to realize that it was all my fears and the way I felt about life. I covered up with my blanket and lay very still, I saw the black horse and it told me to have faith; it was the way to the vision. I felt something get a hold of my ankles and start dragging me off. I peeked out and it was one of the ugly things. I began to pray, but no matter how much I prayed to Christ, it hung on.

"All at once an animal was there, a bear large and strong. 'You are okay,' it said. 'This is only a cleansing and all will pass. Hold on and care about the red balloon.'

"Boy, everything was like I think a drug trip would be like. I looked and there in the night sky was a red balloon. It was night when I saw this but it was a red balloon against the blue sky with white clouds.

"It was quiet for a long time. I thought about the yucky things I had seen and felt. I would feel the fear building, and then the balloon would show up. I felt a peace deep in my mind and was hungry and wanted a bath. Then I saw a path and it was all colors. I walked up the trail and there was a bear and it spoke to me. 'You are home and all will come clear to you soon.'

"I looked up and Cat Eyes was walking towards me. 'You can get your stuff together,' she said, 'and we'll go back to camp.'"

Lee's Vision
"I got to the square and got all set up. I had my prayer flag and blanket and white candle. I wanted so much for this to work and to have

a strong connection to Great Spirit. I wanted to have answers. I wondered if I'd get to understand why my mom died. I spent a long cold time thinking about death and wondering why some people have a good life and others have such a messed up one.

"Sometime in the middle of the next day my mom came to me. I thought it was a dream, but she was so clear and I could feel the kiss on the cheek. I wanted to see her so bad. 'Mom, are you really there?' I asked. She changed into a snake. I was tangled up with the snake and I couldn't move. It was big and strong and there was not one part of me the snake was not wrapped around. It felt like hours before I was free. I spent a lot of time thinking about what it meant.

"Then I was in a rock canyon and a very small woman bundled in a blanket came to me and started talking. She told me that the snake was the excuses I used to avoid my mother's death. I had to walk to the black door and open it. 'What black door?' I asked. The old woman disappeared.

"I sat thinking about how much this square was like the jail cells I had been in. I wondered if that was the black door. I prayed, but it felt hollow and empty just like it always has. I wonder how people can do something that has no feeling. I called on the name of God when I was alone, but there was no one there and no one answered me.

"Sometime in the night a parade of skeletons passed by me and they were screaming and crying. A skeleton stopped and asked me to join them and handed me a cigarette and set a small table up with lots of drugs on it. 'You take all you want,' it said.

"I didn't want anything—just my mom. I cried over all the times in my life that were bad. I sat awake for many hours. I wanted to leave all the bad stuff behind me. And I wanted to run to the peaceful, good life.

"A small white cat came to me and rubbed on my leg—wow, it is hard to tell the difference between spirit and physical!

"'Think about our life, Lee,' the cat said. 'We lose our moms and everything goes on. We don't even know our moms sometimes. Don't worry.'

"I asked the cat if it knew where the black door was and it ran off.

"From the dark, a large bear appeared. It pointed at me and stepped back into the woods. For a long time nothing was going on. 'Til in front of me was a black door. I opened it, and there was another black door that was a hole in the earth, then a black cloud, then a black jail door. This was my vision."

Linda's Vision

"I carried my stuff to my vision square and set up my sacred stuff—drum, blanket, candles, and prayer pole. I got in the square and began to tie prayers. I tied 100 red ties and as I tied them, I thought about what would come during the night. I was full of fear—I never wanted to go camping or be out in the night. When the dark came, I wrapped up in my blanket and shook.

"The fear came 'cause I had a memory I didn't tell anyone. When I was in high school, I had a real good friend who was killed while she was camping, and they never found the person who did it. I was supposed to go camping too, but I chickened out 'cause I was scared of bugs. As night went on, the darkness was all around me and I heard leaves rustling. I called out, 'Who's there?' There were no answers.

"I woke that morning to see darkly dressed men standing all around me—I couldn't see their faces, but they were there. 'Are you spirits?' I asked.

"'It doesn't matter. We have come for you and there is nowhere to go,' they answered.

"I looked away, and there was a lake. I ran to the water and jumped in and when I went under the water, I bumped into my friend—dead and old. The next thing I knew I sat up and was safe in my square. When does this end, I thought. I came to have a vision and this thought of long ago won't let go.

" 'I left the church and came looking for the answers and I will find them!' I said. I filled my time with drumming and thinking. I began to see in front of me a pretty bush with purple flowers, and all around the bush were butterflies—thousands of them—all colors, even green. They were so pretty. I lay back with my head on my arms and the vision was strong—right in front of me. Wow, this is grand, I thought.

"As time went on the bush disappeared. I sat and waited and no bush. Then in front of me lay a large cougar.

" 'Hello,' I said. 'Can you talk? Maybe you can make some sense out of all this for me.'

"The cougar looked at me and said, 'Everything in the Spirit World can talk, 'cause it is in your mind and they are the feelings and words you need to live your life. What do you want to know?'

"I walked over and hugged the cougar. 'How soft and safe you feel!'

" 'Yes, this is what you need to know: Creator loves you and protects you.' he said. 'You have had your vision and now you need to know I'm here to help any time you want.'

" 'I don't remember a vision,' I said.

" 'The bush…' he said.

" 'Oh, yes, the bush, how grand! So that was it—my vision—wow. Now what does it mean?'

" 'That is the work and study that is ahead of you. You will know and all will be clear. The spirits are here to help. Look!' The cougar pointed his paw over to the side of me. There in a soft mist of colors—purple and orange and yellow—were spirits. They were very tall and filled with light and with little dots inside each one of them. There were eight of them and one held out its hand.

" 'Follow, Linda, the answers are with them,' the cougar said.

"As I listened to the spirits, I was to look at the bush and see the answers to my life and the pain and fear I had suffered.

"I looked closely at the bush; as I did, there was an old face in the bush. An old woman, soft and kind.

"'Hello,' the old face said. 'What are your answers?'

"'Answers?' I asked.

"'Yes, how will you get past the fear and anger, the pain and self-abuse you live with from this vision?' the old face asked.

"'I don't know,' I said.

"'Listen, and watch,' the old face said.

The bush was like a TV screen. I could see pictures in the bush like watching a movie. I saw the many people in the world in pain, as my uncle was. I saw there were others like me who were abused, and I didn't feel so alone and victimized.

"'Each time you need answers to questions, look to the bush; you will see the truth and the understanding will come to you,' the old face said.

"I drifted off to sleep. I was on a cloud and slept as I had never slept in my life. When I woke up, I remembered the bush and that I was not the only hurting person in the world. I looked for the bush and there it was. I saw a path, a dirt road with a fence along the road. I felt the fence was keeping the bad away and the path was the way I was to follow. My heart was full of joy and strength: I had my vision."

· 8 ·

Breaking Camp
and Heading for the Lodge

The four students take their journals and start walking toward the tent.

"You will be working in here until you have written everything you need to write about your vision. I am assuming that each of you has a vision, right?"

"I do."

"Yes."

"I do."

"Me too," they all four agree as they follow Butterfly Sky into the lodge. I shake hands with Pepper Dog.

"Our four days are done. I need you to go over the visions," I say to the staff members. "Have each one of them sketch it out, journal their feelings, and then have them load up and head out."

Cat Eyes, the staff member in green, smiles, her eyes twinkling.

"One more time, we've done it, Wolf," she says.

"One more time we see the lost ones find the path," Jack Red Fox says.

"Good job, staff. It's time we gather our things and load up. Break everything down in preparation for the ride home, and as soon as they are finished with their work in the tent, bring that down too. I'll take the jeep and Raven, my half-side, and meet you back at the lodge. Good work."

I load my gear, and Raven, Chimi the wolf, and I return to the lodge. On the drive there, I keep thinking about the wonderment of a vision. I know of nothing in this world that is more satisfying than knowing that Great Spirit has spoken. I remember many times I have seen those smiles and those tears and those sweet looks from the students as they have returned to follow the Rainbow Path, the spiritual road, the Good Red Road, the road of the medicine.

I take a deep breath as we enter the gate at the lodge, and let it out. It's been a long journey. As I get older, I can only think of how nice it would be to go in, drink a strong cup of tea, take a warm shower and go to bed. However, that is not what lies ahead of me. We must place the vision pole in the ground and celebrate the visions.

Each of the students needs time to share. My mind drifts and I hear the wind dancing across the river. I long for those days when I was 19 and stood at the river and looked into the Spirit World. I can smell the campfire and hear the singing voices across the water.

Day becomes night and the moon dances behind the clouds. I watch as seven brightly colored stars dance on the rocks across the river. I follow them, I chase them beyond to the sky above, further out and beyond. I dance with the stars. I look out in front of me and as far as I can see there is deep, dark color with glistening stars underneath my feet. Before me, I see the sun and seven stars cascading down with a crescent moon. It is mine, my vision.

I open my eyes and before me I see the log lodge with its big beams, the beautiful mountains, and the pine trees with the wind whistling through the branches. The beauty of the sun, moon, and stars is my life as a shaman, a teacher, a visionary. I await the students.

As they arrive from their journaling, each one of them has a glow that I recognize.

"Will you join us around the lodge fire and we will talk about the visions?" Cat Eyes asks.

All of us walk over and sit on a log around a soft burning lodge fire.

"How do you feel about your vision quest?" Butterfly Sky asks.

"I can't believe it happened," John replies. "My greatest fears have disappeared. I do have a vision. It's not easy to figure out, but I do have a vision."

"What's hard about it?" Pepper Dog asks.

"It's a road and there are footprints on it and ahead of the road is a bright white light," he says with a bewildered look, scratching his head. "Now what do I do?"

"I find it real important that you begin to understand the sacred discipline of having a vision," I reply. "A vision quest only puts you into position to spiritually experience your mind and your connections to Great Spirit/Grandmother/Grandfather/Creator/God. Life hasn't changed—it's only been enriched."

"Yes," Dancing Spirit, the staff member in purple says, shaking her head. "I can speak to that. When I was in a position of giving up on my physical existence, it was a scary thing because it was all based on my childhood worries, the way the generations of my family had depression through their genes. Everyone was mentally handi-capped and there was a lot of dysfunction. My learning disabilities affected my school years and life was hard. I began to drink in high school. I took drugs in college. Nothing was making sense to me and everything was balling up. Our country was in a time of crisis and everything around me was hard and I decided I wanted to die. Then, I met someone who had gone out on the mountain with Wolf and achieved his vision. It isn't Wolf Moondance who makes a vision happen; it is the calling of your vision itself. I have learned from studying vision quest that it didn't matter if it was in Roman times, Christian times—before or after Christ—in the tradition of the Native Americans, the Celts, the Druids, the Vikings, or whatever. Everyone has a vision. There are many visions in our lives, but my personal vision that connects me to what is true within myself brought me to a place where I can cope with life."

"My vision was hard," Cat Eyes said. "It was a tree with a bird looking out over land. It took me a long time just to figure out what kind of bird it was. When I realized it was a hawk, I studied the hawk and I began to understand that the hawk is a messenger and I began to understand that there are messages in life."

"Yes, that's what happened to me too," White Mouse, the orange staff member says, leaning back on his log and crossing his legs in front of him. "There isn't anything easy about what's going to happen with your visions. There isn't going to be any magical change that happens overnight except that the magical healing has started."

I looked at the questers and I knew it was time to close. The students needed to move on and go forth on the path of their vision. It's always the hardest time, when they come in off the mountain. They have had their sacred vision; they've drawn their pictures and turned them into pictographs, and they've written everything they know about them at this moment in a journal.

"Let me explain to you. As I've told you many times, my vision came when I was five years old, and in this society we don't always get a chance to find our vision when we are five. We don't have the traditional Native American lifestyle that allows us to have our vision quest when we are children and work with it our whole life. We spend too much time today having conveniences and empty religion and educational systems that don't teach about spiritual needs and fulfillment. I can tell you this: as you continue to study about vision questing, you will learn about the deep side of your mind, which is the voice of Great Spirit. Your vision is the site of your spiritual hearing. John, you are on the journey of life. The footprints in your vision may mean that there have been those who went before you. The bright light at the end is hope. I would take that as a simple vision that you should be filled with hope, and that is the message for today from your vision."

John looks at me with tears rolling out of his eyes and he smiles. "There is hope, I can see that in the bright white light and I will hold onto that, Wolf Moondance."

"I want each one of you young questers to know that we will be here for you to help you with your visions.

"Stand up and follow me," I tell the staff and the students.

The staff and questers walk back with me to the lodge vision pole. The staff members remove the burgundy cloths from their arms and give them to the questers.

"Tie the cords to the pole," I instruct them. As they do, I tie an old fork, spoon, and shard of glass to the vision pole. "This ceremony unites us as vision questers. Let no one remove that thought from your mind. We now have our website and there are many people who get online and communicate with each other about spiritual meetings. It's easy—keep writing and keep questioning and keep interpreting. It's time for you as questers to walk into the world and make sense of the vision and the teachings

"Before we go I want to give you each your spirit names. Names come from many traditions. The way I get your names is by listening to your spirit and the Spirit World as you vision and the creator gifts me with a name for you.

"Lee, step up please," I ask.

He walks up to me.

"I see the strength in you; may you walk tall and proud of your experience. Your spirit name is Blackwolf. It speaks of wholeness and the path. You are one to walk the path of wholeness and find the truth and share it with many." I place my hands on his shoulders.

He gives me a hug.

"Many blessings." I say.

"Linda, will you come forth?" I ask. "You are one who has run from the pain, but the running has stopped with your vision. Your spirit name is Looking Wolf. It means one who looks with guidance and sees the truth. You are one who can set the path for others to find their way. As a wolf, you are a teacher," I tell her.

She has tears in her eyes. "Thank you so much, Wolf Moondance," she says.

"You are very welcome. Many blessings."

"Cathy, will you step forward?"

She walks up to me and I look deep in her eyes.

"I see someone who knows herself and the way she is going in life. Your spirit name is Rainbow Wind," I tell her. "It means one who is all, one who speaks the breath of life. Go with many blessings and listen to your vision always," I say.

"John, will you step up?"

He walks up to me, a very soft look in his eyes.

"I see the spirits talking to you and know you can hear them. Many blessings to you. Your name is Strong Elk."

He begins to cry. "My grandfather called me that when I was a boy. How did you know?" he asks.

"Well, John, we do not talk to the spirits for nothing," I say with a grin. "I say so long now and we'll see you soon. Know that we are with you and know that Grandmother/Grandfather/Great Spirit/Creator/God cares and continues to communicate through the voices of the vision."

Aho.

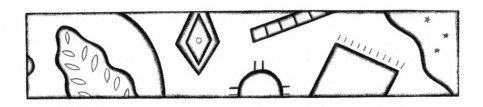

SPIRIT NAMES—WHAT THEY MEAN AND HOW THEY COME ABOUT

I was honored to be a name-giver many years ago. It was a teaching I received from a medicine man in Colorado. I spent a summer studying with him to get the gift of vision of a person's name.

There are many ways a person can get a name. There is the traditional tribal way: someone who loves you and is a good friend gives you a name. Or one who is a visionary sees the name you are called in the Spirit World. Or your name can be given to you by your shaman or a medicine person. Your parents might give it to you at birth or when you turn 21. You may be called to listen to the Spirit World and a spirit names you, or you may just know your spirit name yourself and bring it forth and call yourself by that name.

When I give a spirit name, I feel it is earned. Here are the following things you must do to earn a spirit name:

1. Be true to your self; know you want to live a spiritual life and understand the Spirit World.
2. Be able to see your spirit and understand the Spirit World.

3. Know you are a part of the Spirit World and connect with the spirits daily.

4. Receive your spirit name from a name-giver or as a gift from a loved one, or retrieve your name from your vision.

5. Carry your family clan in your spirit name. Your family's clan name might be Elk, for instance, and your name is Walking Elk.

6. Be able to understand your spirit name and know what it means to you and how it guides you. In the name Blackwolf, for example, black is a color of protection in the Spirit World. Wolf is the teacher, path, or guide. Therefore, you are one who leads others. You are a teacher of wholeness, and protection against all unwanted spirits.

7. You take your spirit name for life, with honor and respect. You place your spirit name in daily use, such as John Bluewolf or Whitehorse Smith, or Mike Walking Elk Daniels. Or your name can be kept silent and only used in spiritual circles and work.

8. You hold the person who gives you the name in high honor.

9. You never fight over your name; you never wish you had a different name, for you are as you are called.

10. You are looking for the truth of the name to guide you and teach you in the Spirit World.

11. You live in a way of truth and spirit. You pray and care for others and live as the name you carry. Study in the Spirit World and about spiritual matters always.

Your spirit name erases old names you have had that might have abuse and pain connected to them. It gives you personal power from the knowing of who you are in the Spirit World. When you have a spirit name, you feel a healing from the old and walk in the truth and the new way of the Creator. Spirit names are very important and bring grand honor.

Finding Your Name in a Vision Quest

To name your self while in a vision quest, look for something you see four times (such as a deer or cougar, a tree or rock), and an action (like standing, running, sitting, or other motion). You also can be called your name by the spirits you meet in the vision, or you can take on a phrase as a name, such as One Who Lives in the Flowers.

When you see some thing four times, like a bear or a tree or a fire, or you hear the wind, you need to remember you have seen, felt, or heard it four times. This will become a part of your name. Then look for an action you do and connect the name, as in *Fox Running* or *White Rabbit Sitting*. Colors seen four times are part of the name. Put the name together and you will know your name when you hear it. There is a deep feeling when you hear your name.

You can take your name from your vision.

Example: You see your vision and it is a flowing river on a clear blue day. You can be called Flowing River *or* Blue Day. *You will know, for the spirit will whisper your name and welcome you.*

I welcome you to call your inner peace and connect with your spirit name. Walk with honor and joy when you are named. After you receive the name, you hold a celebration called a "naming." You invite people over for a meal and sit and share your name. This is a quite joyous accession, not a party. The ones you invite should care about your spiritual experience and name. When you invite them, explain the importance of the gathering and your new spirit name.

Names honor the spirit self and are strong and good. You will grow and heal as you understand the true spirit self.

Aho.

THE VISION POLE

To create a vision pole, you will need:

Tools

&. A pole six to 12 feet (2 to 4m) tall. It can be manmade, a piece of driftwood, or a sturdy, fallen piece of wood that you find.

&. Objects that represent your vision

&. Shards of glass or objects that make noise: pieces of an old wind chime; forks, spoons, or knives; or anything that clangs or rattles

&. Colored yarn in red, orange, yellow, green, blue, purple, and burgundy (you can also find plastic tape in the seven colors at hardware stores)

&. A glass ball (find them at glassblowing shops or gift shops; sometimes called crystal balls)

&. A shovel

&. Cornmeal

&. Tobacco

Your vision pole is to be placed in your yard, usually in front of your home. Sharpen the end of the pole and place it in a hole deep enough to allow it to remain standing upright. If you live in an apartment, I suggest that you fill a large container with dirt—enough so you can plant the pole in it—and place it inside your apartment. Attach your choice of the items above to the pole any way you like.

A vision pole helps you stay connected to your vision. The shards of glass and noisemakers are meant to make connections with the wind spirits. The glass ball is for making connections with the spirit guides and the totems. The colors with which you wrap your pole are there to connect your physical self with the vision.

The color red represents the vision and the confidence to stay connected to it.

Orange is the understanding of the vision, the ability to have balance with the vision and know that your whole life is the vision.

Yellow is the creative connection to your vision that brings forth action, such as writing a book, opening a store, working in communications or at a computer company, or any other creative connections you might have.

Green represents the voice of the vision that reaches out and touches you each moment of your existence from spirit to physicality.

Blue is the solidity of your vision, and the knowledge that when you are lost you can stop, go to a counselor, connect your vision to your daily life, and work your way through any type of dependency.

Purple represents the knowledge that you gain from your vision and the work you put into your interpretations; how much time you take to open the door to spirituality in your daily life.

Burgundy represents the great feeling that you are not alone.

When you look at your vision pole, you know that Grandmother/Grandfather/Great Spirit/Creator is with you; that the elements of fire, water, air, and earth sing the song of life that connects you with your vision.

Take time to build your vision pole, putting everything on it the way you want. The picture here is simply an example. There is no right or wrong vision pole. Everyone's pole is different.

It is important to personalize your pole by placing on it a special hat, shirt, bandanna, or other item that belongs to you. This item on the pole helps you to stay connected, so the symbols of spirit and physicality are never separated. Keep in mind, though, that if your pole is outdoors, the special object will deteriorate.

Place your pole in the ground or in your home with great pride and honor. Go to your pole quite often and sit. Listen to the voice of your vision. Journal your vision and write about it often, bringing forth direction.

Example: You have had problems giving up smoking. You are sitting and looking at your vision pole, and you see the color yellow, the color of creativity. The yellow reminds you that you have the ability to have creativity from your vision. You think of your vision and it is a river, with a fish jumping out of it. All of a sudden, the thought comes to you that if you keep moving and keep going in the right way, you can break any habit. You sit back in your chair, relax and give yourself peace of mind, knowing that you will succeed in stopping smoking. You decide to set an appointment with a physician who can help you with the chemical imbalance that started you smoking in the first place, and you walk forward.

Share your vision pole very carefully with those who ask. Let them tell you what they see and listen, for it may be your vision speaking to you.

Aho.

· 9 ·

Seeing Vision Spirit Guides

I always wonder if the students know the vision is a calling from Creator. I want the purpose to be clear; I want each student to have a clear vision and to find the answers he or she seeks. It is up to the one who quests and to the Creator to have the vision come.

The week after the vision quest, the four students and Pepper Dog, Butterfly Sky, and I meet. We sit around the medicine wheel in the teaching lodge and I start to share with the students the information that will be important to the future of their vision.

"These will be teachings you will want to take notes on, and if you can, please save your questions. Just jot them down in your notebooks and we will answer them when we are done," I state.

"The most important thing in a vision quest is your relationship with your spirit guides. Write in your journal about your animal guides or power animals. Ask yourself, did I find my power animal? Do I have an animal guide? Here are some teachings about your animal guides or power animals, also called animal totems.

"Your power animal is part of a story that connects you and your family to a long lineage on the Earth Mother. You meet the animal in vision. You see the animal four or more times. You may have seen more than one. This is very important to you, for these are power animals, spirit guides. List the animals you have made contact with."

The students are writing and I know this is a good sign.

"You are a total spirit, and physicality is a part of your spiritual life. Physicality is the part of your life that is concrete—the part of your life that is accounted for—the legend of your life. Your physicality is the only thing within your spirit that you cannot control or have any say over—other than to make choices once you are able to make choices in your life.

"You have watched through the eyes of the animals and listened through their ears, for your spirit has always endured within the animal kingdom. The animal kingdom has been here a lot longer than humankind, and your spirit has been in existence a lot longer than the animal kind.

"Before the animal kind, there was an elemental kind, and before the elemental kind, there would have been the celestial kind, and before the celestial kind there would have been pure spirit, and before that, pure energy, and before that, is the point. The point is resonation. So now you can see the lineage of the movement of the point. Existence is the point. Existence became energy, energy became spirit, spirit became celestial, celestial became elemental, elemental became animal, animal became human.

"I hope in the life to come that the voices of the animals are still heard, for when the animals are gone, the elementals will be so sad that they will no longer exist, and the celestial will cease, for its sadness will overcome its life.

"The animals say so many things in their daily routine that are different from human beings. You can talk with your animal guides in spirit or in the physical. It does not matter if you see the animal in the spirit or the physical; the meaning of the animal is still real and applies to your life now.

"In the Spirit World, an animal can speak just like you and me. It is often said that on this earth the animals once spoke. That is true. As spirits they have always spoken, but their spirits were quieted and now can make only noises that are unrecognizable to humankind. But they remember, and if they were to share their memories with us, there might be no more lessons to be learned. So your need for a power animal is exactly what it says—power. The animals hold within them the answers.

"Before I go on, are there any questions about your animals?"

"Does the animal stay in your life always?" Cathy asks.

"It can or not. Sometimes it leaves because the job is done and a new animal will appear. But often your main spirit guide will stay forever," I answer. "Anything else?"

There are no more questions—just eager faces.

"Your sacred council consists of seven animals and you. Picture a circle with seven animals and you in the center. A lot of people say they have an inner totem and four guardians.

"One of the animals in your council is your favorite animal, and that animal is your adventure animal. That animal can change because you can be on a new adventure. So, one day you can have a mouse and that evening, the same day, you could have a bat, and that night you could have a swan. If it is an adventure in dreamtime, the animal may be a swimmer, someone who works in water. Our personalities are based on the movements of our guardian spirits that are animals.

"I often look at myself and teach with my own personality traits. I am a wolf and my elemental is the winter. The reason for that is that the wolf is an elder who belongs to the sacred club of the eagle, the elk, the bear, the wolf, the buffalo, and the cougar. These guys make up . . . shall we say . . . the elder council or the high or strength council. They are the predators, the powerful ones, the strongest. I came to this earth a wolf, and before I was a wolf, I was the winter and before I was the winter, I was from the celestials—the spirits who work with matters of judgment, with rights and wrongs, with cause and effect, with spiritual knowledge and the depth of spirituality. Within the animals is your wisdom."

I ask, "Did any one see more than one animal in your vision?"

Several nod their heads.

"Did you see more than seven?" I ask.

Cathy nodded.

"Good, now you understand why, right?"

"Yes," she says.

I go on. "There is your favorite, which is the shiny part of your personality. The favorite animal will resonate as the shiny parts of your personality, and your favorite animal will stay your favorite animal and that will never change. You resonate with that animal at sleep time. You know that that animal is there for you—it is always watching; it is always taking care of you; it is always there when you need it.

"Then there are your four guardians—the animals of your East, your South, your West, and your North. Those are the animals of your spirit, your emotions, your body, and your mind. They are your guardians. They do that in the development of your life. They will come to you at birth and they will be with you until you become a young person—that will happen at about the age of 12. Then you will receive four new ones, and they will stay with you until you turn 30. Then you will receive a new set, which are your adult keepers.

They will stay with you until you turn 80, and then you receive a new set that will stay with you until you leave. They come on their own. They resonate in your memory but they are there to protect you.

"No one can say what your spirit totems are to you, but you. As you develop your communications skills with your animal totems, you will speak very clearly what they mean to you.

"I hope you have good experiences with your inner totem council of power animals, and that you set out on a quest to learn more information about them through shamanic journeying, by experiencing your inner animal council, by reading and learning about the animal guides you walk with. Questions?"

"Yes," Lee says. "So the animal I have is very important. How do I find the ones in the four directions?"

"You go on a journey to your center and wait for the animals to come. You ask them to show and they will come in order: the first one is the East (spirit); the second is the South (emotions); third is the West (physical); and fourth is the North (the mind). You journal them, then you gather information, and apply it in your life. Understand?" I ask.

"Yep," he says.

"Good. I feel you all have had a good experience with the animal guides of your vision. Now can I hear about the guides you have?"

Lee says, "I have a bear. It is wonderful and knowing, and it talks to me and I can ask it questions."

"Very good," I say.

Cathy says, "My main one is a black horse. That would be my main guide, but there are others, like I said. The bear, a cat and a dog, a fish, a bluebird, and others. I did a lot of writing about them last night and the information you gave us helps. Thanks."

Linda says, "Mine is a soft cougar; he is old and very wise, and I love the answers he has given me."

John says, "It was hard and took a lot of focus, but I have the wolf.

I had to wait and be patient, but when the wolf came, I was told that patience was a lesson I need. The wolf is very right. I look forward to finding the rest."

It has been a good session and I look forward to more.

Aho.

HOW TO MEET A SPIRIT GUIDE

The purpose of a spirit guide is to give you a contact in the Spirit World. Your spirit guide can be a color or a being who is like a human. It can be an animal or even an object, such as a red ball, or a tree or flower. The hard thing about working with a spirit guide is trying to understand the meaning and message the guide is giving. Spirit guides are entities—physical and non-physical—who have chosen to aid others on the path to spiritual enlightenment. Most spirit guides have had incarnations on the physical Earth plane, as well as other realms. Spirit guides can be aspects of yourself.

Guides may remain with you for a lifetime, or come and go, depending on your needs and theirs. They are teachers; they can teach hard lessons or easy lessons. You can ask spirit guides to leave, and they must comply.

We all have spirit guides. The average number of guides is four, usually a mix of male and female. Each guide generally comes in for a specific purpose in your life such as:

1. To be a spiritual guardian

2. To help you heal
3. To help with your creative work
4. To provide spiritual guidance—wisdom and understanding of the human life; to help you realize that you make your choices and they need to be made in goodness and kindness

They may have selected you because they have worked with you in the spirit life or at other times you were on Earth. Or they may be deceased relatives, close friends, or animals—including crawlies, swimmers, and winged ones.

Some guides are your soul mates, which is why you cannot find your true love in the physical. Some guides stay with you for your entire lifetime. Others stay for many years and then leave. In addition to being able to ask a spirit guide to leave, you can ask to have another brought in to help you evolve, if you so choose.

1. When you are in your vision square, you can wait to see if anything comes to you. Just sit and look straight ahead and wait for the sighting. You will see the spirit in your mind or it will look as if it is right there with you. It is sometimes hard to say whether the spirit is right in front of you or not.
2. You can make contact with your guide in a dream or what feels like a daydream. It "speaks" to you in many ways. Sometimes it is the little voice you hear in your head—thoughts. Often it speaks when you are in altered states of consciousness, through art, music, dance, or acting. If it really wants to make a point, it may drop something on you, like a book, as if to say, "Pay attention!"

Spirit guides travel to a human when called or sent by Creator. They come in your spirit journey, dreams, vision, or when you are just thinking.

· 10 ·
"The Sacred Life?"

It is very important to understand that you walk a sacred life after the vision. You have changed from an everyday person to a person with a calling, a person who is listening to the voice of a personal vision. To live your vision you will need Sacred Discipline. It is important that you know your beliefs. Are you Celt, Native American, Wicca, Jewish, or something else? All beliefs call for discipline and they help you fit into your community. When you combine your beliefs with your vision teachings, this gives you your personal life path.

Spiritual life must first be defined and understood. "Sacred" can mean different things to different people and that's okay. I find that shamanism and the Native American medicine wheel concept bring spirituality to form in my life. They provide a really complete understanding of the Spirit World and those who live there. One of the reasons I recommend the Native American medicine wheel—or any type of earth medicine wheel—is because it is a complete connection between the physical and spiritual realms. With an earth medicine wheel, you are studying in a mystery school. Each medicine wheel provides an environment of sacred action.

When you study shamanism or learn in a mystery school that is connected to the Native American medicine wheel, your teachers will bring to your life the principles of discipline, obedience, honor, and respect. When you choose to have sacredness within your life, you are making a decision to separate yourself from a lot of human interactions and temptations that come along in an ordinary existence.

Living as a human two-legged on the Earth Mother, your existence has limits and expectations. Your limits are strictly physical and your expectations are spiritual and physical. To have sacredness in your life, I recommend shamanic journeying and studying all aspects of your vision and how it can affect your daily life. As you get to know your vision, you become stronger in spiritual knowledge and gratitude. It is good to look at your vision as rebirth. As you see your rebirth in your daily life, it will help you use the past, forgive the self, and move on to the will of the vision and the gifts of the spirit.

Vision Quest Rebirth

Each of you has your own reason for going on a vision quest. You may be feeling lost, missing your spirit self, wanting inner peace, looking to heal old pain and wounds. Whatever your initial motivation, a vision quest is a rebirth ceremony. You walk away renewed in spirit and ready to live a new life with a strong spiritual path. Here are the four ways you can know that your spirit has undergone a rebirth.

1. You feel light and free inside.
2. You are full of forgiveness.
3. You want to live life to the fullest.
4. You feel the presence of your spirit guides and want to learn what your vision is all about.

It's a good idea to study your vision each day. Pray for understanding and keep your vision journal close by to write things that come to you in dreams or study. Each day examine the meaning of the things in your vision and turn them into a picture. Then work on understanding the picture and apply the understanding to your daily life. As you work with the vision, the picture around the vision changes, and you can see different things as the vision speaks. Speaking is sight and sight is speaking with a vision. You can hear your vision; we often call that "knowing."

Write in your journal how you are safe because of your spirit guides and the teachings of the flowers, herbs, rocks, and animals. You can grow from your daily connection with your vision because you will learn to have faith and strength and see the beauty and truth your vision holds.

Actions That Oppose Visions

As humankind, you can give up on your vision and think it is not the way to go. There are thoughts that will oppose your vision and stop your vision growth:

1. Selfishness
2. Greed
3. Lust
4. Anguish
5. Mental illness
6. Hatefulness

7. Harboring grudges
8. Revenge
9. Meanness
10. Oppositional attitudes
11. Learning disabilities
12. Fear
13. Jealousy
14. Criminal behavior/stealing/stealing time
15. Going for a vision just to see if it will happen
16. Doing a vision to make a liar of a teacher
17. Wanting to prove the vision is evil
18. Turning to drink and drugs (will weaken and confuse the vision)

These behaviors are all part of being a physical human being. If we want to speak of your flesh and your human existence as being negative and separated from the sacred, these are all good examples. What I would like to share in my personal teaching is that if you look at each one of these behaviors, you will see that they can be changed. As humans, we allow ourselves to believe, much of the time, that these traits are unchangeable, that we're not able to be different, or that we're stuck in these situations.

I like to teach that we have the ability to change all things. I see change as a strong medicine in our lives. We set out to live a full and rich life. Without sacredness, there will be no fullness or richness. The following are sacred actions that can help us overcome the behaviors listed above that might arise in our existence:

Sacred Actions
1. Understanding Grandmother/Grandfather/Great Spirit/ Creator/God.
2. Being in prayer and listening for a return answer. Understand

that, when we pray, we have the opportunity to hear the answer—if we know how to hear the answer. Often we think that when we pray, the Spirit World does not hear. I think that's because we may not know how to listen to the Spirit World. I have often heard people say that when they pray they don't hear anything, or they hear only their own thoughts.

What thoughts did you think you would hear? You know it is all in your head. It is your brain sending signals from your mind to the part of your brain that processes the messages so that you can understand what they mean. Now the tricky part of that sentence is from brain to mind. Your brain is physical but your mind is spirit. What you hear is your thoughts, your voice, but listen beyond that—because in hearing there is a part that is called knowing. When you ask Great Spirit for something and you know the answer and it comes from your voice, you're taught to believe that you're just making up the answer you want—not that it is actually Great Spirit/Creator/God speaking to you. Your brain interprets the signals and sends new signals that form messages from the mind. That is where you're missing the whole structure, if you think you can't hear answers when you pray. You need to have faith that your mind is the realm of spirit and that there are many signals that come through your brain and produce thoughts for you to understand.

Believe that you will hear an answer, and you will. If it comes in your own voice, be grateful that you have an answer. Many times in our lives we overlook the answers, because we are caught up looking for the invisible bearded man who lives in a place far beyond us who is called God and has a special voice that only special people hear. That is a waste of time. Grandmother/Grandfather/Great Spirit/Creator/God speaks to all, and the message comes in a form of knowing.

3. Practicing spirituality and working with religious studies that teach you about the interaction of sacrifice and belief. Sacred actions are ceremonies—times where you structure communication with the spiritual world and sit in reverence of the beauty of nature and the wildlife that lives around you.

4. Studying spiritual teachings, seeking out others' opinions, reading, listening, and deciding what is so for you. When you want to live a sacred life, it is important that you seek out sacred people, look at their lives carefully, and see how they live them.

5. Having a sense of humor. It is necessary to have a good laugh, to feel joy, and to be able to see the delight in children and animals as they play. A smile on your face is proof that you are full of joy.

6. Having a vision. A vision is one of the most sacred things that Grandfather/Grandmother/Great Spirit/Creator/God can give you. Having an understanding of your personal vision will bring forth strength, creativity, power, and impeccability in your life.

7. Having a spiritual routine and ceremony in your life.

8. Having discipline and organization. Discipline and organization are goals, schedules, routines, and methodical behavior. A method in life, with a good schedule, will help you obtain what you set out to achieve. I recommend strongly that you write down actions you plan to take before you take them. When you set goals and write things out, it becomes a sacred commitment and helps you to see clearly and understand what you are about to do. *For example:*

   a. Get married. I know I love this person I have chosen because I can see us happy together in the years to come.

   b. I want to buy a horse because I always see horses in my dreams and I love to be with this animal.

c. I want to move to the state I have chosen because I have job opportunities there.

d. I want to give up my time to serve my vision, because it speaks the truth to me. I can see myself living with the symbols of the vision and knowing where they are leading me.

9. Organizing and living with a journal. You'd think that sacred would come easy, and that it would be an ordinary action in our lives. That might be true if we didn't have choices. That might be true if there weren't an abundance of creativity, or if there weren't material wealth and the potential to gain power on this planet. As sacred individuals, we must apply prayer, journaling, and discipline, set goals, and create schedules to have sacred outcomes in our lives. We are only what we know, and as small children we start to follow those who teach us. If your brain is accustomed to a certain path of thinking, that is the way your brain will go. That is the way you will act in your life. For example, say you see someone hit his hand with a hammer and not make any sound, but just go on doing what he's doing. This could provide a pattern of thinking for a small child that might cause him or her to think that when you get hurt, there is no pain.

It is important to understand that you become who you are by what you see others do. Much of your life plays out because of your brain patterns and not the mental voice of your spirit. From your mind comes your voice, and you know this in your heart because your heart is your mind. You know in your mind. But because your brain patterns what it sees, it will go on doing what it sees. Journaling and the structuring of schedules enables you to have freedom of choice. It is very important for you to have choices and to make changes on a daily basis.

This allows you to see your own patterns of chaos. It allows you to see the chaos patterns of others; it allows you to be in control of your desires, your needs, and your wants. To have organization and discipline, you need to work with a journal.

Start your day by journaling and end your day by journaling. Through this journaling, you build new pathways of thinking. It is important to understand that we are unique and individual only through our needs, goals, and desires. All of us are human and we are all alike in that we can succeed or fail. What allows us to succeed and live a sacred life is that we are organized in going about it.

10. The sacred life includes the following:
    a. Prayer
    b. Ceremony
    c. Journaling
    d. Goals
    e. Discipline to carry out the goals
    f. Achievement
    g. Analyzing
    h. Accepting
    i. Celebrating

I hope these statements will bring some clarity to your concept of sacredness. I strongly believe that when you set up a sacred routine, your life will go in a good way. I would like to share with you these questions I got from working with vision questers and have you answer them in your journal.

1. What is your life?
2. Are you the only one in your life?
3. Why are there people in your life?
4. Who are the people in your life?
5. What are their roles in your life?
6. What kinds of things do you share with the people in your life?

7. What are your hobbies?
8. What is your creative outlet?
9. What causes growth in your existence?
10. What are your truths?
11. What do you believe in?
12. What is your religion?
13. What do you believe spirituality is?
14. Who tells you how to think?
15. Who raised you?
16. What are the things you remember about grade school, junior high, and high school?
17. What were your early sexual experiences, with whom, and why?
18. What do you know about having children?
19. If you have children, how did you raise them and what principles did you teach them?
20. Why do you feel you are who you are?
21. How did you get to be who you are?
22. Who are your elders?
23. Do you know any spiritual people?
24. What does the word supernatural mean to you?
25. What are sacred tools?
26. Do you have any? List them.
27. What is sacred to you?
28. What is wildlife?
29. What is the earth about?
30. Where do you see spirits?
31. How do you talk to spirits?
32. How do you know spirits?
33. Why do you have spirits in your life?
34. Do you have a personal vision?
35. Do you understand the lessons of life?
36. Do you know the sacred laws of existence?

37. What does it mean when you look out your window and see an eagle circle above your house?
38. What is your power animal?
39. What is your inner totem?
40. Why do you believe that herbs and plants exist?
41. What types of spirits do you believe in?

I would like you to buy a 5 × 7 notebook and call it your sacred journal. I would like you to answer these questions in it, and look at who you are and what you know. If you have trouble answering any of the questions, they are topics that you need to study. To obtain, become, and live a sacred life, you have to understand. It is not watching TV; it's not going to movies; it's not making money; and it's not the work you do. It's not the person you are married to; it's not your family members; it's not your children, or your pets; it's not what car you drive; and it's not what you collect, or how many toys you have. It is sacred structure.

Sacred structure is about the spiritual and the supernatural. It is about open, conceivable knowledge. It is about ceremony, respect, honor, accountability, impeccability, discipline, and obedience.

Sacred life includes sacred fire, water, earth, and air. It is about a cycle of energy that is constantly spiraling, and you are a part of that energy. It is about then, a long time ago, now and a long from now, which is the sacred spiral that goes on forever.

Everything in the kingdom of the Earth Mother is part of a story and not just one story, but many stories. There is not one way of knowing or one belief that is absolute. It is beyond. Sacred is shamanic journey—where you go to the Upper World and learn, where you live in the Middle World of reality, and where you go in the Lower World in fear, distortion, and anguish.

Questions to Ask Yourself to Expand Your Vision
1. How do you become sacred?
2. Whom do you ask?
3. What do you study?
4. What is your heritage?
5. What are your principles?
6. What did generations ago mean to you?
7. Why are there different races of people?
8. Where do you see your life changing since you had a vision?
9. Now that you have a vision, what do you do next with your spiritual studies?

You need to step outside of your small, limited life and look beyond. You want a large expansive life, one that you feel good about, one that you feel proud of. Your vision brings grandness to your life. It is a connection between you and Creator. Being with spirit and living a good life is the way of your vision.

Work in your journal and as you come across things that you cannot answer, seek those topics out and understand that the more you allow your mind to expand, the more knowledge you will have.

Sacred Discipline
In the work you have done in your journal, you have begun to know a little more about yourself. You can do many things that will help you in your wish to become a more spiritually developed person. The following are the sacred disciplines I like to teach and live with:

1. Journaling
2. Knowing what kind of person you are (short-tempered, good-natured, big-hearted, kind, etc.). Then you can work with your shortcomings and strengths and use your vision for healing, acceptance, and changing your self.

3. Good lifestyle: healthful diet, sufficient rest, continuing study, solid friendships, pleasant companionship, connection with pets, love of the outdoors, are all good habits to develop.
4. Having faith and the teachings of spirit. Knowing about true spiritual values
5. Learning the sacred spiritual laws and living them in your heart (mind)
6. Daily prayer (knowing whom you pray to and what will happen because of the prayer. Do not just pray an empty prayer, such as God, give me a new car or a million dollars.).
7. Respecting your teachers and elders
8. Practicing spiritual thinking, being mindful of the Spirit World and your guides and guardians
9. Doing ceremony and seeing the outcome
10. Being quiet and respectful, not filled with self
11. Having a personal vision and living your life from its voice
12. Listening to spiritual teachers and knowing the purpose of their lessons in your life
13. Having joy active in your life

Actions to Avoid in a Sacred Way of Life

1. Drunkenness, drug use, eating disorders, and sexual disrespect
2. Living by chance without goals and plans
3. Greed and envy
4. Lies and unfaithfulness
5. Thinking money and material things will make you happy
6. Killing
7. Focusing on or accepting the dark side. (The only "dark" there is, is false control issues of those who are afraid of the truth.)
8. Controlling others because you need someone to hold power over. Often controling people try to dominate others so that their own lives will go the way they think they should.

9. Paying attention to distortion and chaos
10. Wishing harm to others
11. Doing ceremony you don't know the outcome for
12. Stealing objects, power, and time from others
13. Gossiping and talking badly of others

These are actions that tear away at the good energy in your life and turn you away from the Good Red Road (i.e., a spiritual life). As you live with sacred disciplines, better knowledge of yourself and those around you will help you to think in the "medicine way," taking a spiritual approach to life, incorporating the teachings of spirits and words of wisdom from the Spirit World.

Aho.

· 11 ·

Teachings About Sacred Journey
and
a Way to the Spirit Worlds

A Way to the Spirit Worlds

If you want to try this path to shamanic journeying, you will need a personal tape player and headphones, and a drumming tape (or someone to drum for you). You will need some time when you will be undisturbed (turn off the telephone). Ideally, you will be out in the deepest countryside, but this is not always possible.

Be very clear in your mind as to why you are making this journey. Intention is the key to all shamanic work, as energy follows thought. It is worth spending some time getting your intention absolutely clear before you start.

Let's suppose you are journeying to the Lower World to explore. Make the place where you will be working special so that it will aid your journey and you will also be protected (sacred space). Use incense or herbs, cleanse yourself with the smoke. Next, cleanse the room or area you are in. Go to each of the compass points and call in the spirits of those directions, keeping in your mind the qualities that they each hold for you:

The East	*The spirit*
The South	*The emotions*
The West	*The physical form*
The North	*The mind*

Ask them for their help. Speak to the spirits of the place where you are working and ask them to be with you too. Give thanks to all the beings who help you on a daily basis, and for your food, your shelter, your clothes, your spirit tools and so on, and also give thanks to the herbs that you are burning.

Lie down and get comfortable. Spend a bit of time really relaxing and slowing your breathing. Feel the earth under your body taking your weight and supporting you.

Next think of somewhere you have been that feels "earthy" to you—a place where you have felt comfortable and connected with nature. Travel to this place using your imagination. Really feel that you are there; try and sense as much about the place as you can. Look around for an area where you can go down: a hole in the ground, an animal burrow, a hole in the roots of a tree, a well shaft—anywhere you can go down.

Enter the hole and you will typically find yourself in a tunnel that goes downward: it may slope or spiral or drop, but it will go down. You can run, walk, fly, swim, anything you like. Make your way along the tunnel and out into the landscape of the Lower World. Make yourself a promise: that you will accept everything you see and hear with an open heart and an open mind. Your critical mind can have its turn when you get back! Repeat your intention to yourself to focus yourself and to keep you going. Sometimes you may come out into a cave and you will find that you can move easily into the landscape.

When you venture into the landscape, notice as much as you can with your open heart and mind. Feel everything, see everything, notice yourself, whoever else is there, talk to the spirits, and if you feel unhappy about anything at all for any reason, pass it by. Keep restating your intention, if you find your mind wandering. Enjoy yourself!

When you hear the call-back drumming, start making your way back. Retrace your path through the tunnel. You will find that you can float up or otherwise move back up the tunnel easily, and you will come out into the place where you started. Really feel as if you are there, feel the ground beneath you, and then make your way back into your body and into this consciousness.

Record your journeys, as this can be a helpful way of remembering them. Keep in mind that something that may not seem significant at the time may be a useful piece of information at a later date.

Your next journey could be perhaps to find your power animal.

Sometimes your mind wanders during a journey, or you start to doubt what you are seeing, or you judge your performance. This will flip you out of the journey, so restate your intention and pick up where you left off. Sometimes no matter how hard you try, you will not be able to get into the journey. This is okay; it probably means that it is not the right time for you, or you are tired, or whatever. Just try again another time. Trying too hard is a common mistake that people make. It is easier to focus your mind on something, like a place that feels earthy to you, rather than trying to make your mind a blank. Relax and have fun and don't compare your "performance" to others. This is not theater; this is for you and you alone. If you start acting, you are only playing to yourself and preventing yourself from reaching your truth.

After your journey, it is important to close down your space by thinking backward and letting go of all you have worked with. Thank the spirits, those who have been working with you. Go to each of the four directions and say thank you, let go of all the spirits you have met, and take nothing with you in a dream or thought.

Aho.

The Sacred Journey

When we open our hearts and our lives to the companionship—whether actual or symbolic—of spirit guides, our world becomes much larger and richer. Our senses deepen; and as we become aware of how much guides naturally enjoy their contacts with us, we become more comfortable with our own life and vision.

We find ourselves with access to mystery; we begin to let go of the terrible burden of being "human" (not spirit). We are no longer intruders in the world in which we live; we come to care ever more deeply for its other inhabitants. And as we increasingly rejoice in our physicality we find that, like the eagle, we bridge heaven and earth, coming to a total spirit being.

Journeying is a classic technique that is practiced in one form or another by shamans all over the world. It enables us to send our spirits into the Spirit World and is a powerful way of meeting with spirit animals and teachers, finding answers to problems or discovering information and wisdom that can facilitate personal growth and understanding.

A classic way of entering the Spirit World is by using a steady drumming rhythm. This is an old shamans' way and a medicine way of spiritual contact. It encourages theta brain waves that induce the altered state of consciousness required to travel to Spirit Worlds.

The drum is a sacred tool and it has its own spirit. It is used for journeying, healing, and other energy work, as well as singing and chanting (either will raise power!). The drum's own spirit can often be sensed while it is being played, and people sometimes report that they hear other sounds within the drumming, such as music, chanting, and animal sounds. It often seems as if the drumming is coming from all around or from varying directions.

The drum has been referred to as "the shaman's horse," as the shaman "rides" the drumming rhythm to get to the Spirit World. It is like a lifeline, enabling shamans to find their way back quickly and easily. It can also be a timekeeper, as the Spirit World exists outside of time.

There are three main Spirit Worlds; although they are all interconnected, it is easier to think of them as separate for now.

The Lower World is very beautiful and the landscape is a lot like beautiful scenery here in this awareness. Power animals reside here. When you journey to the Lower World, the advice you receive is "earthy," practical, and specific.

The Middle World is the spirit equivalent of the everyday world of ordinary consciousness. You can visit places and times that are important to you, meet with nature spirits, communicate with another's spirit, and so on. It is advisable to become experienced in journeying before traveling to the Middle World, as this is also the place where illness and wandering spirits reside.

The Upper World tends to be somewhat ethereal in nature and you generally meet spirit teachers here who offer advice that is more philosophical and general. As I mentioned previously, all the worlds are interconnected, and you will always meet with spirit teachers and be in the Spirit World that is most useful to you on that journey.

INTERPRETATIONS

The following are ways to help interpret your vision. One of the best ways to understand your vision is through a gut feeling you might have. When you see or hear something in your vision, journal it and then journal your feelings, for this is the strongest understanding there is.

A dream interpretation book may help you figure out some of the symbols. Also look up words in the dictionary that you see and hear: this may help to lead you to the right path of knowledge.

As you receive your vision you may find symbols in it, such as a circle with water drop shapes and six short lines and a chain of interlocking circles. Interpret the symbol by asking yourself what you think of when you look at it.

When you are trying to make sense of your vision, you will want to draw it and listen to your thoughts. You will need to look up symbols. The internet is a wonderful place to find information. So are books about sacred symbols.

SYMBOLS AS KEYWORDS

Symbols quickly fade once the conscious mind begins to kick in, and you therefore need a way to record the symbols as quickly and accurately as possible. Attempting to write symbols down is likely to distract you, and if you're recording your symbols in the middle of the night, it may cause unnecessary sleep disruption. Stick to keywords or short phrases such as "people," "lightning," "green car," "cake."

It is important that you not try to convince yourself that you'll remember the details at a later stage; few people do, and by the time they do, the symbols have often changed significantly. Keep the symbol clearly in mind and journal it quickly. And getting enough sleep is important for a clear vision.

Drawing Your Dream Symbols

Sometimes it's quicker and easier to draw your symbol. For example, you may have met a strange creature in your vision that is half human, half cougar. In such a case, it makes sense to do a quick line drawing. Often this is easier to relate to than a keyword.

Color of the Symbols

Colors often provide important clues. Everybody relates to colors in his or her unique way. For example, if your symbols are red and you associate red with danger, the dream in question may carry a warning message.

Colors also relate to chakras, which can serve as guides to the root of the message. Listed below (on page 163) are the meanings of the colors in our lodge.

Motion and Direction to Your Symbols

Often when we recall symbols, they come in random order. Use arrows to help re-establish the order in which the symbols were presented to you. Add twirls, swirls, or other indicators of motion that will help you keep the vision alive.

If you've recorded your basic symbols while you are in the middle of the vision, place them in your journal and let go of them and go back to the vision. When the vision is done, work with them and add to them until you're satisfied that you've recalled them fully.

Vision analysis requires unorthodox and creative thought. You will be analyzing your vision rather than interpreting it. This means breaking it down into smaller, more focused thoughts and noting your personal association with each vision symbol instead of looking at the vision as a whole. Once you've completed your vision analysis, you will once again bring the symbols together.

1. Understanding emotional response

All feelings experienced within the vision are important, but before exploring individual ones, it will help you to state the overriding effect of the vision in a single word.

Examples: uplifting, discouraging, frightening, enlightening, magical

An easy way to establish this is to imagine that you're relating your vision to another person—your teacher or friend. As you journal it, consider the meaning as if you were describing it for someone else. Without giving it thought, quickly make a statement such as "I had such a _____ vision!" If you're really at a loss to describe the vision in one word, write something like "reminded me of the feeling I had as a child, when _____" or "feels like I have seen this before in my life."

2. Looking at the direction of the vision

There can be moving objects within a vision when you see it at first, as in a movie. Make notes of the general direction of symbols and objects.

For example: fall down into water; climb up a hill; see a lightning bolt. In this case, if your incubated question was about a forthcoming situation, the vision may be saying that it will be something of an up-and-down ride, and not easy.

Common directions of the symbols in your vision that are worth observing are:

up	down
left	right
backwards	forwards
north	south
east	west
horizontal	vertical

3. Quickly responding to individual symbols

Don't try to interpret individual symbols. Instead, pass over the symbols quickly and sift your mind for associations, the quicker the better. Go with gut feelings. What do you think your vision is saying? What do you see in the vision that hits home and gives a clear picture to guide your life? Try to limit your thoughts about the symbols to a maximum of seven words

For example: horse=strength, power, freedom, help, friend, travel, protection

Analysis of the individual vision symbols will follow in the vision interpretation.

4. Looking for common connections

Look at the individual symbols and see if they have anything in common.

For example: all scenes in the vision took place outdoors; all objects were in some way linked with horses; all the characters were male; everybody was facing south; everything was upside down.

There is a common thread within the picture of your vision and symbols. This will help you understand the voice of the vision and hear the message clearly.

5. Recording the vision as a picture
As you have your vision, record it in your journal. Draw the vision in simple form. You do not have to be an artist to have a drawn vision. You can pencil in stick figures, if you have to. Also record the vision in words.

For example: *sun, moon, and stars; seven stars, and the moon was a crescent*

Then look at the vision and start to write your feelings.

For example: *"I see with the sun that I am illumined by my vision. It brings sight to my life. It is a path."*

Bring each thing you see in your vision into word and feeling form and begin to place it in your daily life. Take your time, for your vision speaks in your mind through the spirit voice each day of your life.

On the following pages are basic meanings for some symbols that may appear in your vision.

MEANINGS OF THE ANIMALS

Ant—Patience, teamwork, and cooperation are required

Antelope—Truth; skill

Armadillo—Boundaries

Badger—Energy

Bat—Rebirth

Bear—Introspection

Beaver—Builder

Blackbird—Doing trance work; camouflage

Bobcat—Limits

Buffalo—Prayer and abundance; creativity

Bumblebee—Community; celebration; personal power, courage

Butterfly—Transformation

Canada goose—Sacred circle; failure

Cat—Wholeness

Coyote—Trickster; growth

Crow—Sacred guardian; honoring ancestors; shape shifter

Deer—Gentleness; change; growth; beauty

Dog—Loyalty, unity

Dolphin—Breath of life; prayer

Dove—Peace; sincerity

Dragon—Transformation; warrior

Dragonfly—Illusion, dreams; garden of spirit; beauty

Eagle—Spirit, Great Spirit

Elk—Stamina, strength

Fox—Camouflage; proof

Frog—Healing, clearing, cleansing

Gazelle—Awareness, quick thinking

Hawk—Messenger; vision

Horse—Power, confidence

Hummingbird—Joy; clarity

Jaguar—Solitary path

Ladybug—Ceremony, sacred life; happiness
Lighting bug—Inner peace
Lizard—Dreaming; color
Lynx—Worthiness
Moose—Self-esteem
Mountain lion—Leadership
Mouse—Scrutiny
Mule—Forgiveness
Otter—Woman medicine
Owl—Wisdom; power
Oyster—Filters out life's static; prevents energy loss
Peacock—Wholeness
Polar bear—Integration
Quail—Worth
Rabbit—Warning of fear
Raccoon—Dexterity
Ram—Grandness
Robin—Growth and renewal
Salamander—Transformation
Salmon—Wisdom
Scorpion—Trust; night walker; nightmares
Seal—The inner voice; expectations
Shark—Completeness
Skunk—Self-respect; authenticity, realness
Snake—Transmutation; great feelings
Spider—Weaver
Squirrel—Gathering; reason
Starfish—Understanding
Swan—Grace
Trout—Knowledge
Turtle—Mother Earth; success
Weasel—Discipline

Whale—Record keeper; wise one; sense
Wolf—Teacher; balance

MEANINGS OF THE COLORS

Red—Confidence, strength, nurture, color, accountability
Orange—Balance, success choice, energy, responsibility
Yellow—Creativity, vision, ceremony, prayer, serenity
Green—Growth, beauty, change, courage, honesty
Blue—Truth, healing, proof, understanding, respect
Purple—Wisdom, power, real, knowledge, commitment
Burgundy—Impeccability, great, grand, will, mystery
White—Spiritual
Silver—Spirit
Black—Physical
Gold—Attraction of material wealth

All pastel colors represent spiritual protection of the physical life:
Pink—Acceptance
Pale Orange—Connection
Pale Yellow—Happiness
Pale Green—Discernment
Pale Blue—Drive
Pale Purple—Clearness
Mauve—Joy

MEANINGS OF THE FLOWERS

Depression, Discouragement, Fear—Borage, California wild rose, mountain pride, penstemon, scarlet monkey flower, Scotch broom, star thistle

Making Dreams Come True—Blackberry, buttercup, cayenne, deer brush, filaree, Indian paintbrush, iris, madia (tarweed), Shasta daisy, tansy

Physical Self—California pitcher plant, corn, manzanita, pretty face, rosemary, self-heal, shooting star

Psychic/Spiritual Growth—Angel's trumpet, angelica, black cohosh, California poppy, canyon dudleya, chrysanthemum, forget-me-not, hound's tongue, lady's slipper, lavender, lotus, mugwort, mullein, purple monkey flower, Queen Anne's lace, sage, sagebrush, saguaro, Saint John's wort, star tulip, yarrow

Sexuality, Male/Female Energies, Personal Relationships—Alpine lily, basil, bleeding heart, calla lily, Easter lily, hibiscus, pomegranate, pink monkey flower, poison oak, quince, sticky monkey flower, sunflower

Social Self—Calendula, cosmos, evening primrose, fairy lantern, fawn lily, goldenrod, golden yarrow, larkspur, mallow, mountain pennyroyal, Oregon grape, quaking grass, snapdragon, sweet pea, tiger lily, trillium, trumpet vine, violet, yarrow special formula, yellow star tulip

Stress and Tension—Chamomile, chaparral, dandelion, dill, garlic, Indian pink, pink yarrow, rabbitbrush, red clover, zinnia

Trauma, Avoidance of Feelings—Arnica, baby blue eyes, black-eyed Susan, dogwood, echinacea, fuchsia, golden ear drops, love-lies-bleeding, Mariposa lily, milkweed, nicotiana, Yerba Santa

Vitality—Aloe vera, morning glory, nasturtium, peppermint

MEANINGS OF THE HERBS

African violet—Spirituality; protection

Allspice—Money; luck; healing

Almond—Money, prosperity; wisdom

Aloe—Protection; luck

Amber oil—Love; healing

Apple—Love; divinations; goddess symbol; fertility

Barley—Protection; healing; fertility

Basil—Protection; used to purify circles; as a tea for female health

Bay—Purification; promotes vitality

Blackberry—Prosperity; rest; stress

Boneset—Exorcism; healing

Carnation—Protection; healing

Catnip—Drink the tea to promote sleep, attract a familiar, create love spells

Cinnamon—Love; business; friendship; healing; psychic energy

Chamomile—Money; sleep; love; purification

Cherry—Love; divination

Eucalyptus—Healing; purification

Fennel—Protection; healing; purification

Fern—Rain-making; protection; luck; riches; eternal youth; health; exorcism

Ginger—Energy; strength; passion

Lavender—Beauty; love; peace; protection; dreams, sleep

Nutmeg—Dreams; psychic energy; money

Patchouli—Business; money

Peppermint—Healing; travel

Rose—Protection; creativity; dreams; psychic ability; love

Rosemary—Negative energies; purification; intellect

Sage—Employment, money

Sandalwood—Relaxation, sleep

Thyme—Beauty; courage; health

MEANINGS OF THE STONES

Agate—Brown, gray, and multiple colors. Brings stability to your life due to its hardness and durability.

Amazonite—White or green-blue. Aids the physical body and helps with tranquility.

Amber—Orange, honey, or yellow. Brings warmth to the soul and comfort to those who possess it.

Amethyst—Light lavender to deep purple. It is a primary healing stone due to the six-sided pyramidal point at its end in its natural form. It will also point you in the right direction.

Aquamarine—Pale blue or green, or a combination of both. Calms and relaxes the holder.

Aragonite—Cloudy, milky white or orange. Aids in clearing the senses so that thoughts and emotions can be defined.

Aventurine—Light to dark green. Brings prosperity.

Azurite—Blue-green to dark blue. Promotes healing of arthritis and joint pain.

Bloodstone—Dark green with red flecks. Increases circulation and warms cold hands and feet.

Blue lace agate—Light or dark blue. Promotes peacefulness and clears the mind.

Calcite—Light gray, yellow, or white. This rock gives the holder a sense of direction in life.

Carnelian—Red, orange, or brown. Invokes passion and love; also increases energy.

Celestite—White or light blue. Promotes awareness of the self and surroundings.

Chrysocolla—Light green to deep blue. Helps with protection and insecurities.

Citrine—Light to dark yellow-brown. Brings comfort and calms the self.

Copper—Metallic orange. Transforms thoughts into actions.

Diamond—Colorless, or white, yellow, or blue. This stone is used for courage.

Emerald—Green. Helps with insight and seeing goodness in others.

Fluorite—Pale green to dark purple. Helps to fortify bones and teeth.

Galena—Gray. Helps with circulatory system and improves iron-deficient blood.

Garnet—Black to deep red. Helps the holder to focus on details of everyday life.

Gold—Shiny, metallic yellow. Allows the holder to have a good outlook.

Granite—Multiple colors. Helps in dealing with relationships.

Hematite—Reddish-orange to gray metallic. Strengthens the blood and improves circulation.

Herkimer diamond—Clear. Helps the mind to focus.

Howlite—White with gray flecks. Aids in breathing, especially for those with asthma.

Jade—Green, yellow, or pink. Brings wisdom and prosperity.

Jasper—Red, brown, yellow, or green. Helps to control one's passionate nature.

Labradorite—Blue-gray with other multiple colors. Helps shy people to come out of their shells.

Lapis—Royal blue and gold. Promotes self-importance and confidence.

Leopardskin agate—Brown, orange, or yellow. Allows one to concentrate on life's details and controls metabolism.

Malachite—Light to dark-green. Helps the holder to spend money wisely.

Moonstone—Gray, pearl with color. Associated with love and happy times.

Obsidian—Black, brown, or red. Helps to calm hot-tempered people.

Onyx—Brown, gray, white, or black. Helps to overcome loneliness and unfamiliar surroundings.

Opal—White or colorless. Helps to release anger. Teaches the mystery secrets.

Peridot—Green to yellow. Allows bearer to focus on positive aspects of life.

Petrified wood—Allows one to learn from past mistakes and move on.

Pumice—White or gray. Helps those with weight problems to stick to a diet.

Pyrite—Yellow and shiny. Promotes good health and protects investments.

Quartz—White or colorless. All-around healing stone and brings good luck to the holder.

Rhodochrosite—Pink. Promotes self-acceptance. Helps with remembering dreams.

Rhodonite—Pink with black veins. Promotes positive thinking and helps the holder to overcome difficulty.

Rose quartz—Pink and white. Helps with love and romance. Also helps to improve self-image.

Ruby—Deep red or pink. Protects health, wealth, and body, and strengthens the heart.

Sandstone—Various shades of brown. Helps to clear mistakes. Calls one to work in the legal field.

Sapphire—Blue. Aids good judgment and decision-making. Calls one to be a reporter.

Selenite—Colorless, white, and bluish gray. Helps smokers to quit smoking.

Silver—Shiny silver gray. Aids in blood flow throughout the body. Calls one to work with the ill and walk as a spiritual teacher.

Soapstone—Brown, green, and multiple colors. Promotes change for the body and mind. Calls one to be an artist.

Sodalite—Blue and white. Helps holder to face and stand up to adversity. Helps relieve guilty feelings.

Tanzanite—Blue and purple. Aids in reducing appearance of varicose veins and relieves skin irritations.

Tiger-eye—Yellow, brown, and black. Helps holder to identify and overcome addictions. Calls one to help others stay sober. Will speak of the Good Red Road in dreamtime.

Topaz—Yellow and orange. Prevents procrastination and overcomes the common cold. Calls one to be a physician.

Tourmaline—Many colors. Pink stones help overcome addiction, while blue or green ones heal hernias. Balance between the physical and the Spirit Worlds.

Turquoise—Opaque teal or blue-green. Aids in relieving anger and promotes good luck. Will protect from harm and keep the evil out of your life. Heals fear.

Unakite—Green with some pink. Promotes self-growth, strength, and overcoming

White turquoise—Pale aqua with multi-color veins. Used in ceremony to pray to Creator and Spirit World. Balances the male and female sides in the spiritual.

Epilogue

The students in this vision quest have gone on to make me and everyone associated with the Seven Star Lodge very proud.

Linda Looking Wolf is working in a base camp in Montana with her new husband, Tim. They are working at a lodge and are on the staff of a full-time vision crew. Linda works with the women, helping them understand fear. Her healing work has helped many formerly closed women to open to the spirit ways and receive their vision.

John Strong Elk worked on our staff at the lodge for several years. Then he joined the Marines and has since been serving his country. He is now a commander and plans to remain in the armed services as a life career. He has married and has a son.

Lee Blackwolf has done very well for himself. He finished school and went to the police academy. He works in New York City with inner-city Native American youth who are in prison; he runs vision quests and helps prepare the young people to fit into the norm when they leave prison. Lee comes home to our lodge in the summer and works on vision staff and the vision room on our website, www.wolfmoondance.com

Cathy Rainbow Wind has finished her masters in psychology and has a private practice in Denver, Colorado, where she counsels hard-core alcoholics. She has a wonderful husband, Paul, and a little girl, Skipping Bunny-Cassy. Cathy is also an artist and has her own studio.

Over the years I've had a lot of students matriculate through the Rainbow Medicine teachings and go to vision quest, and they find that they are full and focused and ready to study spirituality. They are open for the voice of the vision to lead them to their dreams and goals. I feel we all need the strength of a vision, for we all need to hear the Creator's voice.

Aho.

Wolf Moondance

To contact the author:
www.wolfmoondance.com

Wolf Moondance
493 East Wonderview Avenue
PMB-170
Estes Park, CO 80517

Index